William Harrison Ainsworth

The Leaguer of Lathom

A Tale of the Civil War in Lancashire - Vol. II

William Harrison Ainsworth

The Leaguer of Lathom
A Tale of the Civil War in Lancashire - Vol. II

ISBN/EAN: 9783337136833

Printed in Europe, USA, Canada, Australia, Japan

Cover: Foto ©ninafisch / pixelio.de

More available books at **www.hansebooks.com**

THE LEAGUER OF LATHOM.

A Tale of the Civil War in Lancashire.

BY

WILLIAM HARRISON AINSWORTH,

AUTHOR OF

"PRESTON FIGHT," "BOSCOBEL," "MANCHESTER REBELS," "TOWER OF LONDON," "OLD SAINT PAUL'S," &c. &c. &c.

'Twas when they raised, 'mid sap and siege,
The banners of their rightful liege,
At their she-captain's call;
Who, miracle of womankind!
Lent mettle to the meanest hind
That mann'd her castle wall.

WILLIAM STEWART ROSE.

IN THREE VOLUMES.

VOL. II.

LONDON:
TINSLEY BROTHERS, 8, CATHERINE STREET, STRAND.
1876.

[Right of Translation reserved by the Author.]

CONTENTS OF VOL. II.

BOOK III.—THE STORMING OF LANCASTER.
(*Continued.*)

II.
	PAGE
THE SPANISH MAN-OF-WAR	3

III.
| ENGRACIA | 21 |

IV.
| HOW DON FORTUNIO AND HIS DAUGHTER WERE RECEIVED BY THE COUNTESS OF DERBY | 27 |

V.
| LOVE AND JEALOUSY | 38 |

VI.
| HOW THE MAYOR OF LANCASTER WAS SUMMONED BY THE EARL OF DERBY TO SURRENDER THE TOWER | 49 |

VII.
| HOW LANCASTER WAS TAKEN BY THE EARL | 60 |

VIII.
| HOW PRESTON SURRENDERED TO THE EARL OF DERBY | 71 |

IX.
| HOW FRANK STANDISH BROUGHT NEWS OF THE SURRENDER OF PRESTON | 83 |

X.

How Hoghton Tower was blown up . . . 91

XI.

How Lord Goring brought a Despatch from the King to the Earl of Derby 97

BOOK IV.—THE SURRENDER OF WARRINGTON.

I.

The Countess proposes to write to Prince Rupert 113

II.

What passed between Standish and Gertrude . 118

III.

How Gertrude accompanied Standish . . . 125

IV.

How Gertrude found her Father at Wigan . 129

V.

How Gertrude warned the Earl that Warrington was in Danger 137

VI.

How Warrington was assaulted by Colonel Assheton and Colonel Holland . . . 142

VII.

How Standish returned from his Mission . . 149

VIII.

How the Earl took his Departure for the Isle of Man 155

BOOK V.—THE BELEAGUERED MANSION.

I.
Of the Garrison at Lathom House . . . 163

II.
How Captain Markland brought a Letter from Sir Thomas Fairfax to the Countess . . 170

III.
How Captain Markland brought a Second Letter from Sir Thomas Fairfax, and in what Manner the Countess replied to it . . . 177

IV.
How Sir Thomas Fairfax came to Lathom House, and what passed between Him and the Countess 182

V.
How a Stand in the Park was destroyed by Rigby, and a Mill burnt 195

VI.
What happened in the Ruins of Burscough Priory 201

VII.
Of the Message brought by Colonel Morgan to the Countess 209

VIII.
How the Intrenchments were made . . . 216   PAGE

IX.
Of the Sortie made by Captains Chisenhale and Standish 224

X.
Of the Important Prisoner brought in by Standish 230

XI.
How the Countess received a Visit from several Royalist Gentlemen 239

XII.
How Rosworm was taken by Standish to the Guard-room in the Gate-house . . . 247

XIII.
In what Manner a Letter was sent to Colonel Rosworm 255

XIV.
A Traitor Punished 266

XV.
How a Letter sent by the Earl of Derby to Fairfax was brought by Captain Ashhurst to the Countess 270

XVI.
How Two Pieces of Ordnance were seized by Standish 275

XVII.
Of the Preparations made for a Grand Sortie . 279

THE
LEAGUER OF LATHOM.

Book the Third.
[CONTINUED.]

THE STORMING OF LANCASTER.

II.

THE SPANISH MAN-OF-WAR.

During a strong south-westerly gale, that had prevailed for two or three days, a large Spanish man-of-war, supposed to be bringing arms and ammunition for the king's party, was driven into the estuary of the Wyre, and blown ashore on the left bank of the river opposite Rossall Hall.

Being unable to get away she fired several guns for assistance, and was quickly visited by a pilot, who found she had sprung a leak, and was likewise immovably embedded in the mud.

At the same time the pilot ascertained that she was furnished with twenty-one pieces of large brass ordnance, and knowing he should be well rewarded for his pains, he made all haste to quit the ship, and conveyed the intelligence to the commanders of the Parliamentary garrison at Lancaster.

Cannon being greatly wanted for the defence of the castle, Major Sparrow immediately gave orders that two or three strong boats should be sent from Sunderland, and taking three companies of foot with him, and a number of men armed with pole-axes, he marched through Garstang, and crossing the Wyre at Saint Michaels, proceeded with all possible despatch to the stranded ship and took possession of her in the name of the Parliament.

The greater part of the crew having already gone ashore, no opposition was offered by Captain Esteban Verderol, and Lieutenant Christobal Puntales, and Major Sparrow and his men immediately began to plunder the ship, carrying off all they could lay hands upon.

All the powder and small arms, together with two demi-cannons, a minion, and three sakers had been got into the boats which had arrived from Sunderland, when the Parliamentarians were disturbed in their operations by a report that the Earl of Derby, with a body of four hundred horse, was coming from Kirkham to attack them.

Not caring to hazard an encounter with the earl, Major Sparrow immediately quitted the ship, and bidding the boatmen proceed to the further side of Wyre Water, here almost as broad as a lake, with the plunder, he beat a hasty retreat with his men.

Only two hours previously had Lord Derby heard of the stranded ship, and feeling certain the Parliamentarians would plunder her and endeavour to secure her guns, he determined to thwart the design.

Accordingly, he set out at once with the force just mentioned, being accompanied in the expedition by Lord Molineux and Captain Standish.

On reaching Rossall, he found several of the crew, and learnt what had happened. Hoping to surprise the rebels, he hurried on, but arrived too late. The enemy had fled, and he deemed pursuit useless.

However, he captured Colonel George Dodding, and Mr. Townson of Lancaster, who had come thither to see the ship, and mistook the Royalists for Parliamentarians.

Lord Derby and Lord Molineux were astounded at the size of the ship, for neither of them had supposed that so large a vessel could enter the mouth of the Wyre, and as she stood there in the shallow water her bulk seemed enormous.

While noting her powerful ordnance, Lord Derby determined to burn her rather than any more of her guns should fall into the hands of the enemy, and Lord Molineux entirely approved of his resolution.

On going on board with Lord Molineux and Standish, attended by a dozen men, he was very courteously received by Captain Verderol, who advanced to meet him, attended by Lieutenant Puntales.

Captain Verderol had already learnt that the new comers were Royalists, and being now made aware that the Earl of Derby stood before him, he addressed him in French, their subsequent discourse being conducted in the same language.

"I am proud to receive your lordship on board my ship," he said. "I regret I cannot offer you a better welcome. Ten days ago, I sailed from Dunquerque, and my instructions from his majesty King Philip the Fourth of Spain, were to land certain arms and stores intended for the use of the Royalist party at some point on this coast. Unfortunately, I have been unable to execute my orders. Caught in a violent storm, I was driven ashore, as you see, at the mouth of this river. Ever since the disaster occurred, I have been unable to communicate with the loyal subjects of King Charles, and this very day my ship has been boarded and plundered by the rebels, who have only just departed, carrying off with them all my powder, and several pieces of ordnance. I would your lordship had arrived a little sooner—you might have punished their audacity as it deserved. Their leader, however, declared that he would return for the rest of the cannon."

"That shall never be, captain," rejoined the earl, sternly. "If the rebels return they shall be disappointed."

"You will take the guns yourself, my lord," cried Verderol. "I am glad to hear it."

"No—that is impossible, captain," said the earl. "The surest way to prevent the guns from falling into the hands of the enemy is to burn the ship. I shall be deeply grieved to destroy so fine a vessel, but there is no help for it."

"If it must be so, it must, my lord," replied Captain Verderol. "I have nothing to say against your determination. You are quite justified in what you propose to do."

"I am of the same opinion, my lord," said Lieutenant Puntales.

"Then let all leave the ship forthwith, I pray you, captain," said the earl.

"Give the necessary orders, lieutenant," said Verderol, stepping aside to hide his emotion.

"See that none are left behind," remarked the earl to Standish, who immediately went below.

On being made acquainted with Lord Derby's intention, such of the crew as remained behind promptly departed, taking with them what they pleased. A couple of chests belonging to the captain and lieutenant were removed at the same time.

Meanwhile, the ship had been set on fire in several places below deck by Lord Derby's soldiers, and shortly afterwards smoke began to appear.

Nothing having been seen of Frank Standish for some minutes, the earl inquired anxiously what had become of him, when the young man suddenly appeared on deck, bearing in his arms a beautiful Spanish damsel of some eighteen or nineteen. She had fainted, and was closely followed by an elderly Spanish gentleman — evidently her father — and a female attendant.

A word of explanation may here be necessary. Don Fortunio Alava, a Spanish merchant trading with France, and his daughter Engracia, with her attendant Maria, were being conveyed from Dunquerque to Cadiz, and had suffered greatly from the disaster that had befallen the ship; but they had been still more alarmed by the visit of the rebels, and had taken refuge in the cabin, carefully barring the door against intrusion.

Not knowing what had taken place, and imagining the rebels were still on board, they refused to come forth from the cabin, and might have been left there to perish, had not Frank Standish burst open the door. Snatching up Engracia, who had fainted, as we have said, the young man carried her on deck, and was followed by the others.

Never had he seen such magnificent black eyes as the fair damsel fixed upon him when she regained her sensibility. She did not thank him in words, but her looks sufficiently expressed her gratitude. What she left unsaid, her father supplied, and as he spoke in French the young man understood him.

At this juncture, Maria uttered a cry, and it appeared that a valuable casket had been left behind. Not a moment must be lost if it was to be recovered, for the flames had already burst forth, and Lord Derby reiterated his command that every one should leave the ship.

Despite the injunction, Standish hurried back to the cabin, but had not returned when Engracia with her father and Maria were lowered into the boat.

Their uneasiness, however, was speedily dispelled by seeing him appear with the casket in his hand, and shortly afterwards, on landing, he had the supreme satisfaction of restoring it to its fair owner.

Pleased by his gallantry, Lord Derby desired him to conduct Don Fortunio and his daughter to Rossall Hall—an order we may be sure he very readily obeyed, and he was delighted to find that he could hold converse with Engracia, since, like her father, she spoke French fluently.

Rossall Hall, which was situated near the sea-shore, was not very far off, and as the party proceeded slowly thither, they often stopped to look back at the burning ship, which now being completely wrapped in flames, formed a very striking spectacle.

"Holy Virgin protect me!" exclaimed Engracia. "Little did I think, when I quitted Dunquerque, that this direful catastrophe would occur!—that our noble ship would be driven ashore and burnt—and that I should be forced to land in England!"

"Instead of repining you ought to thank the saints that you have escaped so well, child," observed Don Fortunio. "But for this brave young gentleman, who preserved us, we should have perished in the flames."

"What a dreadful death!—as bad as an auto-da-fe," exclaimed Maria, in Spanish. "How much we owe the noble caballero! The señorita Engracia must not forget that he hazarded his life to bring her the jewel-case."

"I do not forget it," said the young damsel, fixing her dark eyes upon him.

"You overrate my services, fair lady," replied Standish, who felt the glance vibrate through his breast.

"But what is to become of us in this country?" cried Engracia. "It seems all in a state of rebellion and strife."

"Fear nothing!" cried Standish, with a reassuring look. "You are in good hands. The Earl of Derby will protect you."

"I have heard that the Conde de Derby is the most powerful nobleman in this part of the country, and has several castles," remarked Don Fortunio.

"It is quite true," replied Standish. "Lathom House, the largest and strongest mansion in Lancashire, belongs to him. 'Tis not many days since the queen was there."

"Alas! poor lady! how I pity her!"

cried Engracia. "The rebels, I fear, will never rest till they have driven her from the kingdom, and dethroned the king her husband."

"You take a very gloomy view of matters, fair lady," said Standish. "We confidently expect that the rebellion will be speedily crushed."

"Heaven grant it may be so!" cried Don Fortunio. "My sympathies are entirely with the Royalists."

"And so are mine," added his daughter. "I was afraid we should all be massacred when the rebels took possession of the ship."

"Cielo! how quickly she burns!" ejaculated Maria. "Nothing will be left of her soon."

Again they halted to look at the ill-fated vessel, which was now rapidly being consumed, and were so fascinated by the sight that for a time they could not quit the spot.

It was, in truth, a strange picture. The whole of the crew, numbering three hundred, had now assembled to look their last on the ship, and their cries could be heard at that distance.

Behind them was the troop of horse, drawn up on the bank, and watching the progress of the conflagration with great interest.

At last, it appeared that Lord Derby had seen enough, for his troop quitted their position, and began to move towards Rossall Hall. With him were Captain Verderol and Lieutenant Puntales, who had been provided with horses.

Ere many minutes his lordship overtook Standish, and the party under his charge, and halted to speak to them.

Addressing Don Fortunio, he said: "You will scarce find a refuge for your daughter in this wild and disturbed region. I therefore propose that you should take her to my mansion, Lathom House, where the countess will give her welcome, and where you can both tarry, as long as you think proper."

"I am greatly beholden to your lordship," replied Don Fortunio. "But how am I to get to Lathom House? I am an entire stranger to the country, and, besides, I have no horses."

"Let not that concern you, señor," said the earl. "Horses shall be supplied you, and Captain Standish, with a guard, shall accompany you to my castle."

"Truly, your lordship is a great peer, and report has not exaggerated your princely hospitality," said Don Fortunio, bowing deeply.

Engracia, also, expressed her thanks—but more by looks than words.

Standish could not conceal his satisfaction at an arrangement so entirely consonant to his wishes.

Lord Derby then rode on to Rossall, and the others followed.

On reaching the hall, they found that his lordship had already given the necessary orders, and a couple of horses provided with pillions were quickly brought out.

On one of these Engracia was seated behind her father, while a stalwart trooper took charge of Maria.

A guard of half a dozen men was likewise in attendance.

While taking leave of Don Fortunio and his daughter, and wishing them a safe journey, Lord Derby expressed a hope that he should find them at Lathom when he returned thither.

"Though when that will be, Heaven only knows!" he added, with a melancholy smile. "I have much to do, and my enemies will not be easily overcome. Adieu! To our next meeting!"

"Adieu! my lord," said Don Fortunio. "Never shall we forget your kindness!"

When Standish came to receive the earl's last commands, his lordship said to him in a low tone:

"To-morrow I shall march to Lancaster. You will find me there. Commend Don Fortunio and his daughter to the countess."

"I will not fail, my lord," replied the young man. "I trust to rejoin your lordship ere you reach Lancaster."

He then sprang to the saddle, and putting himself at the head of the little party rode off.

III.

ENGRACIA.

For a mile or so their course lay along the banks of the Wyre Water—a bare and desolate region.

They then struck off towards Poulton-in-the-Fylde, and Standish seized the opportunity of joining the fair Spaniard, whose appearance on horseback had quite enchanted him.

Seated behind her father, as we have described, she looked far better than an English damsel would have done under similar circumstances. But she was greatly aided by her costume. The mantilla covering her jetty tresses, the dark silk dress that so well displayed her symmetrical figure and permitted her small feet to be seen, and the fan she managed so well — all contributed materially to her attractions, and certainly produced an effect upon Standish.

For some little time he rode by her side, and during that interval, he unaccountably slackened his pace. As Don Fortunio rarely made a remark, or looked back at them, they might almost have been alone. What they talked about it is scarcely worth while to inquire, but both seemed interested, and the fair señorita's dark eyes were occasionally cast down and her fan agitated.

Maria, who watched them from her post behind the trooper, came to the conclusion that they had fallen in love with each other, and she was not far wrong.

While passing through Poulton, almost all the inhabitants of which were Romanists and Royalists, many of the villagers came forth to gaze at the foreigners, and seemed wonder-struck by Engracia's picturesque attire and extraordinary beauty. A like sensation was produced at Great Singleton, Wharles, and Treales.

At the latter place, the good folks were informed by a Romish priest that the Spaniards belonged to their own religion, and, in consequence, Don Fortunio was treated with great respect.

Hitherto, they had met with no interruption. Occasionally they overtook a party of billmen or clubmen, but all these stout fellows were going to join the Royalist force at Kirkham, and on beholding Standish and his troop, they shouted

"God bless the king and the Earl of Derby!"

At Tulketh Hall, near Ashton—originally a monastic establishment—the owner of which was a Papist, a brief halt was made, and the Spaniards were very hospitably received.

But Engracia was best pleased by being taken to the domestic chapel by the priest, who resided in the house, and enabled to offer up her prayers to the Virgin.

From Tulketh Hall, half a dozen armed men accompanied the party to the ford across the Ribble — some apprehensions being entertained that a guard had been placed there by the rebel garrison at Preston. However, the report proved unfounded, and they got safe to Penwortham.

Frank Standish had now no misgivings, and would willingly have loitered on the road. But this could not be. On the contrary, he was obliged to push on, in order to make up for lost time.

At the bridge across the Douglas near Tarleton, he perceived three or four Roundhead soldiers, and prepared to attack them, but they galloped off before he came up. He subsequently learnt that they had plundered several farm-houses in the neighbourhood, and were carrying their spoil to Blackburn. This was the only danger to which they were exposed.

Thenceforward, so much expedition was used that in half an hour's time the party came in sight of a large castellated mansion, surrounded by a wide moat, having a great gate-house, turreted walls bristling with cannon, and a lofty square tower in the centre, above which floated a banner, bearing the motto — SANS CHANGER.

Everything indicated that the place was a powerful stronghold.

No remark was made by Standish, but Don Fortunio and his daughter simultaneously exclaimed:

"That must be Lathom House."

"You are right," replied the young man, with a smile. "It *is* Lathom. What think you of it?"

"It is worthy of Conde de Derby," said Don Fortunio.

"It does not appear strange to me," remarked Engracia. "I fancy I have seen it before."

"Impossible, my child," said Don Fortunio. "We have no castle like this in Spain."

"Then I must have dreamed of it," rejoined his daughter.

IV.

HOW DON FORTUNIO AND HIS DAUGHTER WERE RECEIVED BY THE COUNTESS OF DERBY.

As Standish and his troop were recognised by the guard, the gate was thrown open for their admittance, and the party rode in without delay.

The strangers caused as much sensation as they had done at different places during the journey. Officers and men turned out to gaze at the beautiful Spanish damsel.

As yet no news had been received of the destruction of the Dunquerque ship, so they could not comprehend whence she came, but they saw she was a lovely creature, and were glad she had found her way to Lathom.

Amongst the first to notice her was Gertrude Rosworm, who might have been as favourably impressed as the others, if Standish had appeared less attentive, while assisting the fair Spaniard.

From that moment an instinctive feeling of jealousy, for which she could scarcely account, was awakened in Gertrude's bosom.

As to Engracia herself, she was lost in admiration of the mansion.

It chanced that at the time of the arrival of the strangers, the Countess of Derby was in the upper part of the court-yard with her daughters. She had been inspecting some soldiers, and was just about to return to the house, when the Lady

Mary drew her attention to the singularity of Engracia's costume, and she at once exclaimed:

"That must be a Spanish maiden."

Next moment, Captain Standish came up, and hastily explained all that had occurred, concluding with Lord Derby's message to her ladyship.

No sooner did she hear it than she desired that Don Fortunio and his daughter might be presented to her, and received them with great affability and kindness, saying, that as they had been so warmly commended to her by her lord, they were heartily welcome to Lathom. Don Fortunio was much struck by her stately presence and dignified manner, but Engracia felt a certain awe of the great lady.

However, she was charmed with the young ladies Stanley, and felt quite easy with them. They were equally well pleased with her, and thought her the loveliest creature they ever beheld.

After a brief conversation with the strangers, which it is scarcely needful to say was conducted in French, the countess led them into the house, where she again bade them welcome, and signing to Trioche, who was standing among the other servants in the hall, directed him to conduct Don Fortunio to a chamber which she designated in the great gallery.

Her next thought was for Engracia, and being aware that Gertrude Rosworm spoke French, she begged her to take charge of the fair Spanish damsel and her attendant, and find them a suitable bedchamber.

This was soon done, and Gertrude was about to leave them in the room she had chosen, when Engracia besought her to remain.

"Do stay with me a few minutes," she said. "I am sure you are very amiable, and will not refuse to give me some information respecting the castle and its inmates."

"Excuse me, señorita," replied Gertrude. "I am forbidden to talk on such subjects. Lathom House is a garrison."

"Yes, I quite understand," said Engracia. "I have no curiosity to learn how many soldiers it contains—how many cannon—or the amount of its stores. I merely seek a little information on one or two points. First of all I will venture to inquire whether there is a priest in the castle? I am accustomed to have a confessor."

"The countess has two domestic chaplains—Doctor Rutter and Doctor Brideoake, both worthy and excellent men—and service is performed twice a day in the chapel. But these are Protestant clergymen."

"So I supposed," sighed Engracia. And she added in Spanish to her attendant, "You must do without a priest, Maria. There is none here."

Maria uttered an ejaculation of despair.

"There may be a priest for aught I know," remarked Gertrude. "If so, you will soon hear of him. Two of the officers and several of the men are Papists."

"I hope the caballero who brought us here is not a heretic?" cried Engracia.

"Captain Standish is a Protestant," rejoined Gertrude.

"Ay de mi!" ejaculated the devout Spanish damsel, clasping her hands.

"What matters his faith to you?" cried Gertrude, sharply.

"Nothing," replied Engracia.

But her looks contradicted her words.

"If you would stand well with the countess do not talk to her on matters of religion," said Gertrude. "She is not tolerant. With this piece of advice I leave you."

And she quitted the room.

"I do not like that damsel," observed Engracia to her attendant, as soon as they were alone. "Nor do I think she likes me."

"The señorita is right," replied Maria. "The maiden's eyes had a jealous sparkle in them. Do not trust her. She regards you as a rival."

"As a rival!" exclaimed Engracia.

"As sure as I was born in Cordova, she is in love with the handsome caballero," pursued Maria.

"It may be so," said Engracia, colouring deeply.

"The señorita need not trouble herself about that," cried Maria. "She is preferred, I am certain. I saw enough during the journey to convince me the caballero is desperately enamoured of her."

"But he is a heretic, Maria."

"The señorita will convert him."

"The difficulty is great—but perhaps it may be got over," said Engracia.

"No doubt of it," replied Maria.

"De paso, what have you done with the casket, Maria?" inquired Engracia. "I hope you have not lost it?"

"Lost it! Saints forbid! It is here," cried Maria, producing it.

Engracia was gladdening her eyes with a sight of its glittering contents, when a tap was heard at the door, and some girlish voices called out in French, "May we come in?"

Conjecturing who were her visitors, Engracia opened the door herself, and beheld the young ladies Stanley, who had brought her some articles of attire, thinking she might need them.

"I am sure my dresses will fit you," cried Lady Henriette Marie. "We are about the same height."

"You are a little taller, but they will fit me perfectly," replied Engracia.

"They will become the señorita maravillosamente," cried Maria, as she took the dresses.

"How can I thank you for this great attention!" cried Engracia.

"We want no thanks—we want no thanks," cried all three girls. "It is a pleasure to us to serve you."

Suddenly Lady Kate caught sight of the casket, and exclaimed:

"Heavens, what beautiful jewels!"

"Where?" asked the little Lady Amelia. "I don't see them."

"There—on the table," replied Lady Kate.

And they all rushed forward to look at them.

For a few minutes nothing was heard but rapturous exclamations.

Charmed by this display, Engracia in the most obliging manner begged each of them to select an ornament.

"Oh! no—no—no!" they all cried, drawing back.

"You will deprive me of a great pleasure if you refuse," said the good-natured Spanish maiden.

"But we can't possibly accept such magnificent presents," replied the Lady Henriette.

"Will you deign to accept a single pearl each?" said Engracia.

The two younger girls consulted their elder sister by a look.

While they hesitated, Engracia took three pearls from a string, and gave one to each.

"I would willingly do more, if you would allow me," she said, smiling.

"You have done far too much already," rejoined Lady Henriette. "These are lovely pearls. We must show them to the countess, our mother, and if she will allow us, we will gladly accept them."

They then retired, but the little Lady Amelia would not quit the room till she had kissed her new friend.

Contrary to expectation, the countess did not object to the gifts. Like her daughters she was charmed by the winning and ingenuous manner of the fair Spaniard, and would not mortify her by a refusal.

V.

LOVE AND JEALOUSY.

The countess had been questioning Standish as to her lord's plans, and though she naturally felt some anxiety as to the result of the meditated attack on Lancaster, she allowed no doubt to appear in her looks.

"If Lancaster falls, Preston will soon ollow," she said; "and then my lord will once more be master of that part of the country. Of late, the rebels have been gaining ground, but a defeat like this will be a great check to them. I am sorry his lordship felt compelled to burn that Spanish ship."

"The step was unavoidable, madam," replied Standish. "Had the rebels succeeded in securing the guns, Lancaster might have held out for a month."

"But what has become of the unfortunate captain and his crew?" inquired the countess.

"The captain and lieutenant are with his lordship," replied Standish. "As to the crew they will doubtless join our ranks."

"When do you return?" she demanded.

"Not till to-morrow," he replied. "Horses and men will then be fresh. I shall set out at daybreak, and hope to rejoin his lordship near Lancaster."

"It is well," said the countess. "You shall take a letter from me to him."

Just then, her daughters entered the

hall, and showed her the presents they had received from the fair Spaniard.

"She is as generous as a princess," observed the countess, smiling.

"I hope she will remain with us a long time," said Amelia. "I am sure I shall love her very much."

"Yes, we all like her," said Lady Kate.

"I do not wonder at it," remarked the countess. "But she may not wish to remain here."

"I think she does," said Lady Henriette.

The hour had now arrived at which the countess attended evening service in the chapel, and she therefore proceeded thither with her daughters. She was followed by Standish and several of the household, and Gertrude soon afterwards joined the little train.

The chapel was situated in the inner court, and was capable of containing a great number of persons. A large pew on the left near the altar was occupied by the countess and her daughters. Gertrude sat with them. The body of the chapel near the door was crowded with musketeers, in front of whom were Captains Standish, Chisenhale, Ogle, and Molineux Radcliffe. The service was admirably performed by Doctor Rutter.

When the congregation came forth, Standish repaired to the stables to give some orders to his men, and was returning through the inner court, when he perceived Gertrude at a distance and tried to overtake her, but she hurried on, and avoided him.

According to custom supper was served at eight o'clock in the great banquet-hall. Among the company were Don Fortunio and his daughter, with all the officers of the garrison. Don Fortunio sat on the right of the countess, and Standish contrived to obtain a place near Engracia. Gertrude was likewise present, but she sat at the other end of the table, and never looked towards them.

Both chaplains supped regularly with the countess, and grace was never omitted before and after the meal. Great form was observed on the occasion ; the servants were marshalled by a steward carrying a wand, and Trioche devoted himself exclusively to the Spaniards.

But the meal, though ceremonious, was of short duration. When grace had been said by Doctor Bridcoake, the countess arose, and all [the company followed her example.

For some time the party remained in the hall, conversing together.

After pacing to and fro for a few minutes, Standish and Engracia sat down on a couch at the further end of the vast apartment, which was here but imperfectly illumined. They had much to say to each other, but now they were alone, and might have said it, they remained mute.

"Why are you so pensive?" inquired Engracia, at length.

"I am thinking how wretched I shall be to-morrow, when I am forced to ride away," he replied. "For the first time the battle-call will fail to animate me. Yet I should not feel so sad, if you would give me some hopes that the passion you have inspired is requited."

Owing to the obscurity, Engracia's blushes could not be seen, and besides she had her fan. She murmured some response, but it was scarcely audible. Standish took her hand, and as she did not withdraw it, he conveyed it to his lips.

"You have wrought a great change in

me," he said. "Heretofore, I enjoyed nothing so much as an expedition like that in which I am about to be engaged, but now I would rather stay here."

"That must not be," she cried. "Go and fight by the side of your valiant lord, and win renown. You may be certain I shall think of you constantly during your absence, and rejoice at your return."

"I shall find you here when I come back?" he asked.

"Undoubtedly," she replied. "There is no probability of our immediate departure. The countess, as you know, has seconded her lord's invitation, and urged us to stay as long as we like. She is a noble dame. I am delighted with her and her daughters, and feel I shall be happy here."

"I am glad to hear it," said Standish. "I feared this dull life would not suit you.

There are no diversions here—no fêtes. One day is like another."

"I do not want amusement. I shall think of you. I should have been perfectly content if there had been a priest."

"That is a difficulty I cannot get over," said Standish. "But I would recommend you to perform your devotions in private—since by doing so, you can offend none."

"Such is my design," said Engracia. "I spoke to the damsel who conducted me to my chamber, and she gave me like advice."

"Gertrude?" remarked Standish.

"Yes, that is her name. She is very beautiful, and I cannot but admire her, but I do not think I can ever love her."

"I hope you may not dislike her," said Standish. "I fear she dislikes you."

"Why should she dislike me? What have I done to offend her?"

"Nothing," replied a voice near them, which both recognised as Gertrude's. "I heard my own name mentioned," continued the speaker, "and I deem it right to say I have no feeling towards you save good will."

"I am glad to receive the assurance," said Engracia.

"Do not confide in her," whispered Standish.

"I fear I have intruded, but I have no such design," said Gertrude.

Then addressing Standish, she added, "The countess desires to speak with you. She is in the presence-chamber."

"I will attend upon her ladyship at once," he replied.

And bowing, he left the two damsels together.

Proceeding to the presence-chamber, he

found the countess. She gave him a letter, and charged him with several verbal messages to the earl.

"Say everything loving from me to my lord," she observed, "and all that is fond and dutiful from my children to their father. I have but one other injunction to give you. Be first to bring me tidings of the defeat of the rebels."

"If life be left me, and my lord will grant me leave, I will do it," replied Standish, as he placed the letter carefully in his doublet.

"You set out early in the morn?"

"At daybreak."

"'Tis well. A soldier should be early. I have only to wish you a good journey, and a safe return. Au revoir."

No other opportunity occurred to the young man of exchanging a word with Engracia, beyond bidding her adieu at parting for the night, but the tender valedictory look she gave him was sufficient.

He looked round in vain for Gertrude. She had retired.

The bell struck five as Standish entered the court-yard next morning, and found his little troop waiting for him, fully armed and equipped.

It was only just light, and the musketeers were scarcely distinguishable on the walls, but while glancing round, he perceived a female figure near the entrance of the hall, and feeling sure it must be Gertrude, he left his horse with a trooper, and hastened towards her.

Before he could reach the spot, the figure had disappeared.

VI.

HOW THE MAYOR OF LANCASTER WAS SUMMONED BY THE EARL OF DERBY TO SURRENDER THE TOWER.

No adventure of any kind occurred to Standish and his troop till they came within a few miles of Preston, when learning that the bridge over the Ribble was strongly guarded, they turned off on the right, and crossing the river near Walton-le-Dale, proceeded to Ribbleton, and thence to Fulwood and Broughton.

The whole of this district was overrun by foraging parties from Preston, and being anxious to avoid an engagement, Standish sought to keep out of their way; but as he drew near Myerscough Hall—the residence of Sir Thomas Tyldesley, who was then with Lord Derby—he encountered a small troop of Parliamentarians.

They had been plundering some farm-houses belonging to Sir Thomas, and were hastening to Preston with their spoil. Standish at once attacked them, and a sharp conflict ensued, but it was soon ended. Shouts were heard in the direction of Myerscough announcing pursuit, whereupon the Roundheads threw down their booty and galloped off.

Immediately afterwards a dozen stalwart yeomen, mounted on strong horses, and armed with muskets and pistols, made their appearance, and were well satisfied to regain their goods without continuing the pursuit. They heartily thanked Standish for the aid he had rendered them, and only wished they had come up in time to punish the robbers.

From these men Standish learned that the Earl of Derby had arrived overnight at Garstang with the whole of his force, and was probably there still. But for this piece of information, a halt would have been made at Myerscough, but the young man now pushed on, and in half an hour reached Garstang, where he found Lord Derby, who was very glad to see him, and receive the letter from the countess.

Before eight o'clock, the whole Royalist force, now exceeding three thousand men —horse and foot— set forward towards Lancaster. The men were in good spirits, and enjoyed the march.

Mists still hung upon Bleasdale Moors, and the Fell Ends overhanging Lower Wyersdale, but the estuary of the River

Lune and the broad expanse of Morecambe Bay glittered in the sunbeams.

Ere long, the stern old keep of Lancaster Castle came in sight, and on beholding it, the billmen and clubmen shook their weapons and shouted lustily.

From their numbers the Royalists presented a very imposing appearance. The advanced guard, consisting of three troops of horse, was commanded by Lord Molineux. Then came Lord Derby at the head of a large body of horse, very well mounted and equipped. These were followed by several companies of musketeers, led by Sir John Girlington and Sir Thomas Tyldesley. Then came Sir Gilbert Hoghton with a regiment of horse, while the billmen and clubmen, divided into fifteen companies, each numbering a hundred, and each having a captain, brought up the rear.

These formidable fellows were content

THE STORMING OF LANCASTER. 53

to serve without reward, but expected to pay themselves with plunder. Embodied with them were the crew of the Spanish ship, armed with pikes, and commanded by Captain Verderol and Lieutenant Puntales.

On arriving at Moorside, within a mile of Lancaster, a halt was called, and Lord Derby, attended by Standish, rode to the front to reconnoitre the town, and confer with Lord Molineux and the other commanders.

Lancaster Castle, as already explained, was fortified and garrisoned by a strong Parliamentary force, commanded by Colonel Holcroft, Major Sparrow, and Major Heywood, and could only be taken by a regular siege, but Lord Derby intended to storm the town, and deal with the castle afterwards.

His lordship was much surprised, however, to find that, after all, the guns had been recovered from the charred remains of the Spanish ship, and transported to the castle walls, where they now threatened him, but though vexed, he could not help admiring the spirit displayed by Major Sparrow.

In addition to the force of the garrison, two regiments had been formed by the townsfolk, each three hundred strong, and respectively commanded by Captains Ashworth and Shuttleworth.

Until the arrival of the Earl of Derby, the Parliamentary commanders were very well satisfied with their preparations, but when they beheld the large Royalist force drawn up in the plain below, they began to feel uneasy, and messengers were despatched to Sir John Seaton at Preston, urging him to send them aid.

Having carefully examined the defences

of the castle, and pointed out the Spanish guns on the walls to Lord Molineux and the others, Lord Derby read to them a summons, which he proposed to send to the mayor and burgesses before commencing an attack on the town. Thus it ran :

"I have come to free you from the bondage of the declared traitors, who now oppress you, and seek your destruction by bringing you into their own condition. Deliver up your arms, and lend me aid to regain the castle, and you shall have all fair usage. If not, expect from me what the laws of the land and of war will inflict upon you."

This missive, being entirely approved by the other commanders, Lord Derby delivered it to Captain Standish, who immediately rode off towards the town, attended by a trumpeter carrying a flag of truce.

On arriving at the entrance of the town, Standish found a small troop of horse drawn up under the command of Captain Shuttleworth, who rode forward to meet him, and learning that he brought a summons for the mayor from the Earl of Derby, said:

"If you will tarry but a short space, I promise you shall take back an answer—but to obtain it you must accompany me to the castle."

"The answer I require is from the mayor and burgesses," said Standish. "The commanders of the garrison are not summoned. Lord Derby well knows they would not surrender the castle. The town is different."

"The mayor and the town council are now in the castle with Colonel Holcroft," replied Captain Shuttleworth. "They will consult together when the summons is laid before them."

"On that understanding I consent to accompany you," said Standish.

Thereupon, they proceeded to the castle, followed by the guard.

At that time Lancaster Castle was surrounded by a moat, and had been strongly fortified by the Parliamentarian commanders. The walls were thronged with musketeers, and amongst its ordnance could be discerned the pieces of cannon taken from the Spanish ship.

While Captain Shuttleworth passed through the gateway to deliver the summons to the commanders of the garrison and the mayor, Standish remained outside, near the drawbridge, and employed the interval in surveying the magnificent prospect spread out before him. His eye was still wandering over the estuary of the

Lune, Morecambe Bay, and the fine Westmoreland hills, when Captain Shuttleworth came forth, and giving him a letter, said:

"This is the answer to Lord Derby's summons. I will tell you its purport. The mayor and burgesses affirm that the castle never was at their command, and having been taken and fortified by the Parliament, the Parliament now holds the town in control. Thus much on their part. But even if the town were independent of the castle, they, the mayor and burgesses, would never consent to a surrender."

"They understand the consequences of a refusal, I presume?" observed Standish, sternly. "They must expect the full punishment of war."

"They will adhere to the Parliament, and resist to the uttermost," replied Shuttleworth.

Standish said no more.

Accompanied by his conductor to the end of the avenue leading to the town, he took a courteous leave of him, and rode back to Lord Derby.

On perusing the answer brought him the earl was highly incensed, and exclaiming that the rebels and traitors would bitterly rue their decision, gave immediate orders for the assault.

VII.

HOW LANCASTER WAS TAKEN BY THE EARL.

In a very short space of time, the whole Royalist force, divided into four squadrons—each numbering four hundred men—was moving towards the town, but in different directions, as the attack was intended to be made at various points.

Besides these, there were the billmen and clubmen, who were likewise divided into four companies, each having a mounted leader.

The squadron commanded by Lord Molineux started first, having a wide circuit to make, and kept as much as possible under the cover of the hedges, but it was descried from the castle, and formed a mark for the guns, which now began to play upon the besiegers.

Moving off with his men towards the river, Sir John Girlington attacked the town on the north. An intermediate point was chosen by Sir Thomas Tyldesley, while Lord Derby marched along the high road on the south side of the town. Not only was he exposed to the fire of the castle guns, but his advance was disputed by Captain Shuttleworth and a large body of cavalry.

Seeing that a charge was about to be made, the earl halted, and firmly received the furious onset.

He then attacked the rebels in his turn, and drove them back into the town, killing a great number, and pursuing them so quickly that they could not make another stand.

In vain Captain Shuttleworth endeavoured to rally his men. They would not stop till they reached the castle, and being hotly pursued by Standish and a party of horsemen better mounted than the rest, Shuttleworth was cut down before he could cross the drawbridge.

This daring act had well-nigh cost Standish his life. A shower of bullets flew around him, and it seemed miraculous that he was not hit.

However, he managed to rejoin Lord Derby safe and sound, and found him engaged in setting fire to several houses in the main thoroughfare, in order to clear them of the marksmen, who did great mischief.

Meanwhile, the rattle of musketry was

heard in other quarters, commingled with the roar of the castle guns. But the latter did more harm to friends than foes, and many buildings were crushed by the ponderous shot.

Strange to say both Captain Verderol and Lieutenant Puntales, who were with Lord Derby, were killed by the discharge of a cannon taken from their own ship. Their death infuriated the crew to such a degree, that they butchered many unresisting townspeople, and vowed vengeance upon Major Sparrow.

They kept their oath in this manner. Three of them, armed with muskets they had picked up, contrived to reach the bank of the moat unobserved, and perceiving Major Sparrow on the walls, whom they recognised from having seen him when he plundered the ship, they took deliberate aim, and shot him.

By this time, the town was completely invested by the Royalists, who gained an entrance at every point they attacked, and driving their opponents before them made their way to the market-place, where they formed a junction.

In accomplishing this object they sustained comparatively little loss, but the destruction they caused was terrible. The Parliamentary troops who opposed them were forced to retreat, while the towns-people, many of whom were favourably disposed towards the besiegers, were ruthlessly slaughtered, since no quarter was given. Buildings were set on fire in every direction, and two whole streets were burnt down, but not before the houses had been pillaged by the billmen and clubmen, who claimed the right to plunder.

For more than three hours the Royalists

were scattered in various parts of the town, and as they could not be restrained by their leaders, the havoc was frightful.

Such were the horrors of Civil War, like excesses being committed by both sides.

During all this time, the guns of the castle continued firing, but as we have already explained they did infinitely more damage to the townspeople than to the enemy.

At length the strife ceased, at least in the central part of the town. Quarter, hitherto refused, was now given in every instance, to those who submitted. Houses were still burning in various parts, and pillage was still going on, but the firing from the castle had ceased. Indeed, there was good reason for the cessation, for the supply of powder was well-nigh exhausted. This circumstance would have rendered

Colonel Holcroft seriously uneasy, if he had not felt sure of aid from Preston.

No intelligence had been received from Sir John Seaton, but it could not be doubted that when that brave commander heard of Lord Derby's attack upon Lancaster, he would hasten to the assistance of the town and garrison.

Lord Derby was quite aware of the difficulties in which the garrison was placed. He knew they not only wanted powder and match, but provisions, since several hundreds of the townspeople had taken refuge in the castle, and must be fed. He also knew that the well would soon be drained, and the want of water and food must compel a speedy surrender.

He therefore determined to press the siege with the utmost vigour, and was detailing his plans at a council of war held in the town-hall, when a sudden change was caused by important intelligence brought him by his scouts from Preston.

That very night it appeared Sir John Seaton was about to march from Preston with fifteen hundred musketeers and some troops of horse to the relief of Lancaster.

Lord Molineux, Sir Thomas Tyldesley, and the other commanders and captains who assisted at the council, looked aghast, but Lord Derby seemed quite undismayed.

"Since Sir John Seaton is coming to Lancaster, we must go to Preston," he said; "but by a different route. Doubtless, he will march through Garstang. Our route must, therefore, be by Cockerham, Kirkland, and Catterall. We will set forth at dusk with our whole force."

"It will be dark in an hour, my lord,"

said Sir Thomas Tyldesley. "The men are scattered about the town, and cannot be got together in that time."

"They must," said the earl. "Preston must be attacked to-night, and before dawn it will be in our hands."

"A bold stroke, and I doubt not it will prove successful," observed Lord Molineux.

"Deprived of all its strength, the town can offer no resistance, and must surrender," said Sir John Girlington.

"Ay, the Royalists will not be afraid to declare themselves," said Lord Molineux.

"They will welcome us as deliverers," said Sir Gilbert Hoghton. "Sir John Seaton could not have served us better than by this movement."

"'Twill be a good exchange," said Lord Derby. "Preston is of more importance to the king than Lancaster; and having recovered it, we will summon Blackburn."

"Nothing would please me better than to punish that insolent town," said Sir Gilbert Hoghton.

"Ere many days you shall have the satisfaction you desire, Sir Gilbert," rejoined the earl. "But, first, we must secure Preston. Let the men be got together forthwith. But mark! no trumpets must be sounded; or our purpose will be suspected, and information sent to the enemy."

"Tidings of Seaton's design cannot yet have reached the garrison," remarked Lord Molineux.

"I will not answer for it," replied Lord Derby. "But if Colonel Holcroft finds we have quitted the town, he will infallibly pursue us, and endeavour to impede our march."

"We ought not then set out till it is quite dark," observed Sir John Girlington.

"We must quit the town by different outlets," said the earl; "and our rendezvous must be Ashton, on the left bank of the Lune. Now to collect the men."

VIII.

HOW PRESTON SURRENDERED TO THE EARL OF DERBY.

By dint of great exertion on the part of the commanders and officers, the men belonging to each corps were got together at the appointed time, and marched secretly out of the town, as Lord Derby had directed.

The chief difficulty was with the billmen and clubmen, who were very reluctant to abandon their spoil, but being told that they would certainly be cut to pieces if found there by Sir John Seaton, they contented themselves with what they could carry off.

Lord Derby was the first to arrive at the place of rendezvous, but the others were not long behind.

It was now dark, but from this point the town presented a terrible spectacle. Many houses were still burning in various quarters, and a lurid light was thrown on the walls and keep of the castle.

Dreadful as was the scene, it produced little effect upon the beholders, most of whom rejoiced to think that Sir John Seaton would find the town untenable on his arrival.

As soon as the force was complete, the order to march was given.

Lord Derby commanded the advanced guard, and Sir Thomas Tyldesley brought up the rear. The road to Cockerham was taken, and as they were now close to the bay, and the tide out, the broad sands could be distinguished through the gloom.

Nothing occurred till they reached Cockerham Moss, and as they skirted it, the sound of horse was heard behind, and they knew they were pursued.

On this alarm, Sir Thomas Tyldesley halted, and immediately wheeling round, awaited the horsemen, whom he did not doubt came from the castle.

Lord Derby's departure had not been accomplished with so much secrecy as to escape the notice of the garrison, and Colonel Holland finding that the whole of the Royalists had evacuated the town, and probably set out for Preston, started in pursuit with a large party of horse, determined to harass them.

Easily ascertaining the route they had taken, he hovered for some time in their rear, and then made a sudden dash forward, but Sir Thomas Tyldesley being prepared, drove him back with the loss of several men, and the colonel did not hazard another attack.

Thenceforward, the march of the Royalists continued without interruption.

From Nateby, Frank Standish, ever ready for a daring exploit, rode across the country with a couple of well-mounted troopers and brought word back that Sir John Seaton with his whole force had halted at Garstang.

It had been Lord Derby's intention, as we have shown, to surprise Preston that night, but as he proceeded, he learned from his scouts that the Royalists had begun to display a bold front against the few Parliamentarians in the town, so that he should be able to take possession of it almost without a blow. He therefore postponed the attack till the morrow, and halted for the night at Fulwood Moor, on the north of the town.

The inhabitants, however, soon learnt that he was in the neighbourhood with a large force, and the tidings being quickly spread about—notwithstanding the lateness of the hour — caused the greatest delight to the Royalists, and corresponding dismay among the rebels.

It chanced that there were several Roundheads from Blackburn and Bolton lodging at the inns that night, who sought to decamp, but were unable to do so, since the ostlers, who sympathised with the Royalists, locked the doors of the stables, and took away the keys, to prevent the intending fugitives from getting out their horses.

Next morning, at an early hour, Lord Derby marched up to the Friar's Gate. The avenue was strongly guarded, but not a single shot was fired, and as the earl drew near with his whole force, the rebels fled.

The bars were then broken down, and the gate burst open by the clubmen, whereupon several troops of horse dashed in, and galloping right and left, posted themselves at Church Gate and Fisher Gate to prevent flight, while another party scoured the Ribble Bridge and the adjacent ferry.

Meanwhile, the earl had entered the town with his commanders, and after ordering several arrests to be made, and a great number of houses to be taken possession of, but not plundered, he proceeded along Friar's-street at the head of a regiment of horse.

Crowds of loyal folk came forth to greet him—hailing him as their deliverer. All the Parliamentarians seemed to have disappeared. Scarves and kerchiefs were waved from the windows, hats flung in the air, and enthusiastic shouts were everywhere heard of " God bless the king and the Earl of Derby!"

Thus triumphantly did the earl ride to the market-place, where a large concourse was assembled.

Before alighting at the town-hall, he called to Standish who was close behind him, and said:

"Take half a dozen men wth you, and make all haste you can to Lathom. Tell the countess I have recovered Preston for the king, without a shot fired or a life lost. The news will gladden her."

Standish instantly set forth on the joyful errand. He was the first to quit the town, and cross the Ribble, since gate and bridge had been guarded by the Royalists. As he looked back from the river-side, he saw the royal standard floating above the church tower.

Lord Derby's orders were strictly carried out. Anxious to avoid a repetition of the terrible scenes that had occurred at Lancaster, he would not allow any slaughter.

Several hundred prisoners were made, and being deprived of their arms, were shut up in the church or in the gaol.

Finding it impossible to check the clubmen, Lord Derby allowed them to plunder a certain number of houses and shops, and then dismissed them.

Heavy fines were imposed on several of the wealthier rebels, and were ordered to be paid at the town-hall on the following day, and the amount was then distributed among the soldiers.

When Preston was stormed by Sir John

Seaton, Adam Morte, the loyal mayor, was slain while fighting valiantly against the besiegers.

His grave was in the churchyard, and all the prisoners taken to the church were compelled by Sir Thomas Tyldesley to walk past it bareheaded.

Not deeming this indignity enough, the guard would willingly have forced them to kneel down at the grave, while some of the townspeople, who revered the memory of the heroic mayor, went still further, and would have shot a score of rebels on the spot.

"In losing Adam Morte, we lost the best and bravest man in Preston," remarked a bystander. "He was a staunch Cavalier, and detested a Roundhead as much as he loved the king. He vowed he would never surrender Preston with life, and if the besiegers entered, it should be over his dead body. The first three Parliamentarians who mounted the walls fell by his hand. He could have escaped with his men, but he would not fly. He fought obstinately to the last—wounding a rebel with every blow. Mad with rage against him, they thrust him through with their pikes, and flung his bleeding body from the walls. And here the brave man lies. Shall we not bedew his grave with their blood?"

Had the guard received a look from Sir Thomas Tyldesley they would have complied, but he sternly shook his head.

"Adam Morte fell in fair fight," remarked one of the prisoners—a dark-looking Puritan.

"Thou art one of those who helped to slay him, Phineas Clay," cried the first speaker.

"I deny it not," rejoined Clay. "I glory

in the deed. I did good service in removing so bitter a malignant."

As the words were uttered, a bullet was lodged in the Puritan's brain, and he fell upon Adam Morte's grave.

No one knew by whom the shot had been fired. Nor did Sir Thomas Tyldesley care to inquire.

Lord Derby and Lord Molineux took up their quarters in the town-hall. Sir Gilbert Hoghton owned a large mansion in the town, which had been occupied by Sir John Seaton, while he was in command of Preston.

Of course, Sir Gilbert took immediate possession of his own house, and Sir Thomas Tyldesley and Sir John Girlington were lodged with him. There was no difficulty in providing the soldiers with quarters.

Plenty of ammunition was found in the magazine, and on the walls, which had recently been strengthened by Seaton, were a few small pieces of ordnance. This was highly satisfactory to Lord Derby, since it was quite possible he might soon be besieged in his turn.

IX.

HOW FRANK STANDISH BROUGHT NEWS OF THE SURRENDER OF PRESTON.

ABOUT noon on the same day on which Lord Derby regained Preston, the countess ascended the Eagle Tower at Lathom House, in company with her daughters, Gertrude Rosworm, and Doctor Rutter. She conversed with none of them, and her countenance wore a thoughtful, almost sad expression.

Early that morning a messenger had brought word that Lancaster had fallen;

adding that half the town was burnt and many of the inhabitants slain.

The latter part of the intelligence distressed her exceedingly, and she could not shake off the painful impression.

"Your ladyship looks pensive," observed Doctor Rutter.

"I am thinking of Lancaster," she replied. "Much mischief must necessarily be done when a town is stormed, and if the soldiers only suffered I should not much heed, but I cannot help grieving for the inhabitants who have been forced by the garrison to resist. I am sure my lord would willingly have spared them, had it been possible."

"Rebellion must be punished with severity, madam, or it can never be effectually crushed," replied the chaplain; "and though no doubt many innocent persons perished with the guilty in this terrible siege, the earl could not distinguish between them. The blame must rest with those evil-minded persons who compelled their fellow-townsmen to defy the king's authority. 'Tis to be hoped that the fate of Lancaster will prove a warning."

"The warning, I fear, will be disregarded," said the countess. "The rebels will retaliate. The castle is still occupied by the garrison, and will cost a long siege ere it can be taken."

"In my opinion, madam, the garrison will surrender," rejoined Rutter. "The capture of the town is a great blow. We shall soon hear more good news."

"It comes!" cried Gertrude, who had been anxiously looking out for another messenger. "I see a small party of horsemen galloping hither."

All eyes were instantly turned in the direction towards which she pointed.

"You must be mistaken, girl," said the countess. "I can perceive no horsemen."

"You will behold them presently, madam," replied Gertrude. "They are hidden by the trees."

Almost as she spoke, the troop appeared, and the Lady Henriette Marie called out:

"Yes, there they are! The Cavalier at their head is Captain Standish."

"Standish!" exclaimed the countess. "Then, of a surety, he brings good tidings."

"Was I not right, madam?" said Doctor Rutter. "I doubt not the castle has been taken."

"Surrendered—not taken," rejoined the countess. "I am heartily glad of it."

Just then the leader of the little troop, which was approaching very rapidly, descried the party on the Eagle Tower, and waved his feathered hat to them.

The action caused great excitement among the beholders, and the young ladies Stanley, as well as Gertrude, waved their kerchiefs in reply.

"May we go down and meet him, dearest mother?" said the Lady Henriette Marie.

Beseeching looks were cast by all the others at the countess, who willingly assented, and the whole party descended to the court-yard.

By the time they got there, Standish and his followers had nearly reached the mansion, and a loud shout from the warders at the gate, and musketeers on the walls, greeted them, as they crossed the drawbridge.

Perceiving the countess and those with her in the court, Standish hastily alighted and hurrying towards her would have flung himself at her feet if she had not stopped him.

"Your news—your news?" she cried.

"My lord has recovered Preston," he replied.

"Indeed!" she exclaimed, in astonishment. "When I last heard of him, he was at Lancaster, and about to besiege the castle."

"His lordship left Lancaster last night, madam, and this morning, he surprised Preston. He is now master of the town."

"A great achievement, and quickly performed," she rejoined. "It will redound to his lordship's honour." She then asked in an anxious tone, "Has there been much slaughter?"

"None whatever, madam. His lordship bade me tell you that not a man has been killed."

"I am truly glad to hear it. This clemency may be set against the havoc at Lancaster."

"His lordship would gladly have spared the people of Lancaster, madam; but they refused his summons, being compelled to do so by the commanders of the garrison."

"Had the garrison been put to the sword I should not have grieved," said the countess; "but I pity those poor souls."

"They do not all deserve your pity, madam — nor can they complain, since, as I have shown, they brought this punishment upon themselves."

Here Doctor Rutter interposed.

"Shall we proceed to the chapel, madam," he said, "and offer up thanks to Heaven for the victory vouchsafed us, and for the preservation of the earl from his enemies?"

"I was about to make the suggestion, reverend sir," said the countess. "Our first duty is to Heaven, and if we neglect it, we cannot hope that our cause will continue to prosper."

By this time, all the officers of the garrison had come up, and manifested the greatest satisfaction, when they learnt that Preston had been recovered.

X.

HOW HOGHTON TOWER WAS BLOWN UP.

COLONEL NICHOLAS STARKIE, of Huntroyd, a staunch Parliamentary leader, who had previously defeated Sir Gilbert Hoghton at Hinfield Moor, having learnt that Sir Gilbert had marched with Lord Derby on Lancaster, resolved to surprise Hoghton Tower, and suddenly appeared before it with three hundred men, and some cannon, and firing a shot against the gates summoned the commander to surrender.

Captain Musgrave, who had been left in charge of the castle by Sir Gilbert, and had with him forty musketeers, haughtily refused the summons, and at once returned the fire.

The defence was vigorous, but it soon became clear that the assault would be successful, whereupon Captain Musgrave sent out an officer to demand a parley, which was granted.

A conference then took place between Musgrave and Colonel Starkie—the result of which was that the former offered to deliver up the castle, provided the lives of the garrison were spared.

These terms being agreed to, after the delay of half an hour, Colonel Starkie and his men entered the outer court, where they found Captain Musgrave with the musketeers drawn up, and ready to depart. The great gates of the inner court were likewise thrown open, and no one could be seen upon the towers or walls.

"You have done wisely in delivering up the castle to us, Captain Musgrave, since you cannot hold it," said Colonel Starkie, as he courteously saluted the discomfited officer. "You have made a gallant defence."

"I hope Sir Gilbert Hoghton may think so," replied Musgrave sternly. "Are we free to depart?"

Receiving an answer in the affirmative, he passed with the musketeers through the outer gate, and quickly descending the hill, made the best of his way with the little party to Walton-le-Dale, whence they proceeded to Preston.

Meanwhile, Colonel Starkie entered the castle with his men, and mounted towards the upper part of the building, in quest of arms and ammunition.

In a chamber on the summit of the structure, they found a much larger supply of muskets, calivers, petronels, and pistols than they expected, besides a great number of old arquebusses.

Moreover, there were two or three barrels of gunpowder, one of which seemed to have been half emptied by the men previous to their departure, since a good deal of powder was scattered about on the floor, and on the staircase.

Attaching little importance to this circumstance, Colonel Starkie was collecting all the arms he could find, when a terrific explosion took place, that shook the whole fabric to its foundations, rent the walls, blew off a large portion of the roof, and scattered great beams, stones, and mutilated bodies far and wide.

Immediately following the explosion,

shrieks and cries could be heard, forming altogether a most appalling and unearthly noise.

When the soldiers left in the court-yard recovered from the shock, they rushed into the house, and found nothing but a heap of ruins, amidst which could be seen the bodies of their dead or dying comrades.

The upper part of the staircase was entirely destroyed, the floor cracked and broken, and a great portion of the roof blown off.

It was speedily discovered that a train had been laid, which had set fire to the barrels of gunpowder.

By this stratagem Colonel Starkie with a hundred and fifty of his soldiers were destroyed. Starkie's body was so mutilated that it was only by his accoutrements that he could be recognised. The train had been laid by Urmston, the steward. He was betrayed by some of the household, and shot.

The central part of the edifice, where the explosion occurred, was so damaged that it could not be inhabited, and it was not thought worth while to repair it. But the castle was fortified as strongly as ever, and the three large pieces of ordnance still kept their places on the outer gate.

By the Royalists the act was looked upon as just vengeance—by the Roundheads it was regarded as a detestable piece of treachery, which Heaven in due time would infallibly punish.

XI.

HOW LORD GORING BROUGHT A DESPATCH FROM THE KING TO THE EARL OF DERBY.

Two days after he had captured Preston, Lord Derby held a council of war in an inner room in the town-hall, at which Lord Molineux, Sir Gilbert Hoghton, Sir Thomas Tyldesley and all the other commanders were present.

"I have now a proposition to make to you," he said. "This success must be immediately followed up. Before the rebels can recover from their surprise we must strike another and heavier blow. We must attack Manchester with the fixed determination of taking the town. I doubt not we shall be successful. This very night we must start on the enterprise. If we tarry here we shall have to defend ourselves against Sir John Seaton and Colonel Holcroft, who most assuredly will besiege the town, whereas if we set out at once our movements cannot be checked."

"I entirely agree with your lordship that it will be best to leave Preston," said Sir Thomas Tyldesley; "but I thought it was your intention to take Blackburn, and then proceed to Bolton."

"Manchester is far more important than either Blackburn or Bolton," rejoined the earl. "And if I march against the town now, I will either take the place, or lay my bones there. Are you of my mind, gentlemen? Will you all go with me?"

"After our former experience," remarked Lord Molineux, "I think the attempt on Manchester very hazardous——"

"The town must be captured—sooner or later," said Lord Derby, "or the whole county is lost to the king. At this moment, Colonel Holland and Colonel Assheton are unprepared."

"Well, I will raise no further objections," said Lord Molineux.

"I will go wherever your lordship chooses to lead me," said Sir Thomas Tyldesley.

"And I," added Sir Gilbert Hoghton, and several others.

"Then we will set out to-night with all our force," said the earl, "and proceed to Chorley. To-morrow we will move on to Wigan, and give out that we mean to assault Bolton, but ere another dawn shall break the rebels shall find us at Manchester."

Preparations were then secretly made by the Royalists for their departure, and at nightfall, Lord Derby, with his whole force, marched to Chorley, where they took up their quarters for the remainder of the night.

After a few hours' repose, the army pursued its march to Wigan without meeting any opposition.

This town still remained faithful to Lord Derby, and here he had placed a strong garrison under the command of Major Blair, and had recently fortified it with new gates and outworks, so that the town was in an excellent state of defence, and the commander laughed at the threats of the rebels.

But scarcely had Lord Derby entered Wigan than all his plans were frustrated.

Lord Goring, with a small guard, had just

arrived from Oxford, bearing a despatch from his majesty. The earl received him in the presence of Lord Molineux and all the other commanders.

"You are welcome, my lord," he said. "I trust you bring good news from his majesty?"

"Not such good news as I could desire, my lord," replied Goring. "The king has instant need of aid, and enjoins your lordship, on your allegiance, to send him forthwith all the men you can spare. The despatch I have just given you is an order to that effect, as you will find. Lord Molineux is also commanded to rejoin his majesty with all his officers and men."

"I am quite ready to obey the order, my lord," said Lord Molineux; "though I must mention that I have engaged with Lord Derby to make another assault on Manchester."

The earl was unable to conceal his chagrin, though he controlled himself as well as he could.

"I am ready as ever to obey his majesty's behest," he said; "and will bring him all the troops I can muster—horse and foot. But I must pray for three or four days' delay, during which I shall endeavour to take Manchester; and the importance of that capture will, I trust, satisfy his majesty."

"There must be no delay, my lord," said Lord Goring, haughtily. "You make sure of taking Manchester, but you were not successful on a former occasion. As I have already told you, his majesty requires at once all the force he can muster."

"My lord, I believe if I had an opportunity of speaking to his majesty, he would approve of my purpose——"

"Then you refuse to obey?" said Lord Goring, sternly.

"No, my lord, but I must strongly remonstrate," said Lord Derby. "An opportunity will be lost that may never occur again."

"I am bound to say," remarked Lord Molineux, "that, in my opinion, Manchester is so strongly garrisoned, and so well defended, that it cannot be taken under a month."

"You hear, my lord?" said Goring, looking at the earl. "How say you, Sir Thomas?" he added, to Tyldesley. "You have had experience of this rebel town."

"My experience leads me to the same conclusion as Lord Molineux," replied Sir Thomas. "Manchester cannot be taken by a *coup de main*. Colonel Holland and

Colonel Assheton are too much on the alert."

"You are both mistaken," cried the earl, warmly. "Let us march there to-day and I will engage to take the town before to-morrow morning. If your lordship will come with me, you shall behold the royal banner floating from the church tower at dawn."

"I cannot comply with your request, my lord," replied Goring. "Nor can I permit troops, that will be invaluable to his majesty at this juncture, to be sacrificed in a useless enterprise. I must be frank with your lordship. Neither the king nor his council think you are serving the royal cause in Lancashire.

"Not serving it!" exclaimed the earl. "What would you have me do? I have just taken Lancaster and Preston."

"But you can hold neither place," said Goring. "And I am certain his majesty would not sanction your proposed attack on Manchester. I have commissions for Lord Molineux and Sir Thomas Tyldesley, empowering them to recruit their regiments from your last levies, and to join the king immediately at Oxford."

"Since such are his majesty's commands I shall not oppose them," said the earl; "though I feel I should best serve him by acting contrary to his orders. However prejudicial to the royal cause it may be to strip Lancashire of its defenders, I am ready to take my whole force to Oxford."

"That is not needful, my lord," said Goring. "The king desires you to retain such troops as may be necessary, but to send him all you can spare."

"I will take them to him as I have just said," replied Lord Derby.

"My lord," said Goring, "it will suffice if Lord Molineux and Sir Thomas Tyldesley join his majesty. Hereafter, if required, you can follow. You are best here for the present. Lancashire must not be given up to the rebels."

"If I lose my men, I can make but a poor defence against the enemy," said the earl. "But his majesty shall be obeyed. My men are ready to march in another direction—but it matters not. They will go wherever I bid them, and though I doubt not they will regret as much as I do myself that the attack on Manchester is abandoned, they will fight well elsewhere. I will take my whole force to Warrington, where I will leave it at his majesty's disposal."

"Nay, my lord, I must take the greater part of it with me," said Goring. "Such are my orders."

"You shall take all if you will," rejoined Lord Derby.

"A dozen troops of horse and five hundred foot will suffice for the present," said Goring.

"You shall have them," replied the earl. "As soon as the men have rested, we will set out."

Two hours later, the whole force that had just arrived at Wigan set out for Warrington.

As Lord Derby had anticipated, the change in the plans gave great dissatisfaction, and much reluctance was expressed by some of the soldiers to proceed to Oxford.

During the whole of the march between Wigan and Warrington, Lord Derby rode by himself. A short halt was made at Newton, but even then his lordship seemed in no humour for converse. Evidently it was a great grief to him to part with his army, and he could not conceal his vexation.

The whole force rested that night at Warrington, but early on the following morning, the chosen regiments set out for Chester on their long march to Oxford, under the command of Lord Molineux and Sir Thomas Tyldesley.

Thus checked in his victorious career and deprived of the greater part of his force and his two most efficient commanders, Lord Derby could not but feel the greatest mortification and disappointment.

Overcome by a despondency he could not shake off, he remained for three days at Warrington, when news was brought him of a great disaster.

Wigan had been captured by Colonel Assheton with a very strong force, consisting of upwards of two thousand men, and the town plundered.

Immediately on receiving this grievous intelligence, Lord Derby put himself at the head of the two troops of horse which were all that were now left him, and rode off to Wigan to see what could be done.

With him was Captain Standish, who had only joined on the previous day. The second troop was commanded by Sir Gilbert Hoghton.

On the earl's appearance before the recently captured town, the fortifications of which showed how much it had suffered from the recent assault, Colonel Assheton immediately sallied forth at the head of a force trebling that of the Royalists.

A very sharp conflict ensued, during which many were slain on both sides, but at length the earl was compelled to retreat. He did so, however, in very good order, and rode with his company to Lathom House.

End of Book the Third.

Book the Fourth.

THE SURRENDER OF WARRINGTON.

I.

THE COUNTESS PROPOSES TO WRITE TO PRINCE RUPERT.

NATURALLY, the unexpected return of the Earl of Derby to the castle under such circumstances caused great consternation.

The whole garrison got under arms. As soon as his lordship had ridden through the gate with his followers, the drawbridge was raised, and preparation was made for attack.

After dismounting in the court-yard, the earl immediately retired with the countess, and told her all the reverses he had sustained—how he had been thwarted in his intended assault of Manchester—how his best troops had been taken from him—and how Wigan had been captured.

"Wigan captured!" exclaimed the countess, in amazement. "I heard it had been attacked—but I knew not it was taken."

"It was taken yesterday by Colonel Assheton, and is now in the hands of the rebels," replied the earl, despairingly. "Only Warrington and this stronghold are left me. All else is gone."

"Do not despair, my dear lord," she said, striving to cheer him. "Fortune will take a turn."

"I fear not," he replied. "Things will get worse, instead of better. Warrington is certain to be attacked by the rebels, but it is well fortified and well garrisoned, and may hold out for a time; but if the whole county is in the hands of the rebels, I cannot maintain it. As the king will not have me with him, I must perforce retire to the Isle of Man."

"Not yet, my dear lord—not yet," remonstrated the countess. "All is not lost. I will write to Prince Rupert to come to our assistance, and I doubt not he will accede to the request."

"You are mistaken, my dear heart. Goring and Jermyn, and the rest of the king's advisers, who are hostile to me, will not let him," observed the earl.

"Nevertheless, I will write," she said; "and I will send the letter by Frank Standish."

"A better messenger could not be found," rejoined the earl. "If the prince will bring a sufficient force to Lancashire, all will be right. But I fear——"

"Have no fear, my lord," cried the

courageous dame. "All will yet be well. Go forth, I pray you. See your children. Show yourself to the officers of the garrison. I will join you as soon as I have written the letter to Prince Rupert."

Very much cheered by his discourse with the countess, the earl proceeded to the great hall, where he found his daughters with Doctor Rutter, and embraced them tenderly, and then cordially greeted the chaplain.

After this, he went forth into the courtyard, where all the officers of the garrison were assembled.

Putting on as cheerful a countenance as he could assume, he thus addressed them:

"You have heard we have just lost Wigan, and it is doubtless a very heavy blow to us, and a great gain to the rebels, but rest assured we shall recover the town. Meanwhile, we have Warrington, which is strongly fortified, and which we can hold till we receive assistance from the king."

"I hope the assistance may not be delayed, my lord," said Captain Chisenhale.

"When his majesty learns how we are situated, I trust he will send Prince Rupert to our assistance," said the earl.

These words, and the tone in which they were spoken, produced an excellent effect on the officers, who had been much depressed by the loss of Wigan.

The earl next carefully inspected the whole garrison, and by his manner inspired confidence in the men.

II.

WHAT PASSED BETWEEN STANDISH AND GERTRUDE.

Meantime, Frank Standish had gone in quest of Engracia and her father.

But before he could find them, he encountered Gertrude.

"I grieve to hear you have lost Wigan," she said.

"Yes, the town was taken yesterday by Colonel Assheton, with the aid of your father," he replied, gloomily.

"Was my father with Colonel Assheton?" she inquired.

"He was," replied Standish.

"I am sorry for it," she rejoined. "But do not reproach me. I am not to blame."

"The rebels will attack Warrington next, and your father may give them further aid."

"Yes, I see, that is possible," she replied. "I will try to prevent it."

"What will you do?"

"I will go to Wigan and talk to him. Perhaps he may listen to my entreaties."

"That is not very likely. But the countess will not allow you to leave Lathom House on such an errand."

"I will find some means of getting away," she replied.

"Do not come to any decision till you have spoken further with me," he rejoined.

At this moment, Engracia was seen approaching with her father, and Standish went to meet them.

"Ah, my young friend, I rejoice to see you," said Don Fortunio. "But is it true you have sustained a reverse?"

"Yes, we have lost an important town," replied Standish; "and one I thought perfectly safe. All our late successes will now go for nothing. Warrington alone remains to us."

"And this castle," cried Engracia.

"Yes, but if Warrington falls, Lathom House will be besieged," said Standish. "Do you think you ought to remain here?"

"I am not at all afraid," she replied. "I feel quite safe with the countess."

"You do not know what a siege is like my child," cried Don Fortunio. "The matter requires consideration. Would it be possible to quit the castle now?"

"Yes, but a few days hence it may be too late," replied Standish.

"I do not wish to go, dear father," said Engracia. "If you desire to depart, leave me here."

At this moment the countess appeared with her daughters. She had a letter in her hand.

"I was looking for you, Captain Standish," she said. "You must take this letter to Prince Rupert."

"To Prince Rupert!" he exclaimed in astonishment. "Unless I am misinformed, his highness is at Oxford with the king."

"It is to Oxford you will have to proceed," replied the countess. "If you deem the journey too long, I will send another messenger."

"The journey is not too long for me, madam," he replied. "If I have my lord's consent I will willingly take the letter."

"His lordship has selected you for the errand," said the countess.

"Then I will set out at once," replied Standish.

"I felt sure I could rely on you," she rejoined, with a smile. "You will deliver this letter into the prince's own hands as speedily as may be, and bring me back an answer."

"I will, madam," he replied, placing the letter in his doublet.

Just then Lord Derby came up, and finding that the countess had already entrusted her letter to Standish, he took him aside, and charged him with a message to Prince Rupert.

"You will be able to describe to his highness the exact state of affairs in Lancashire," he said. "Tell him I deem it utterly impossible to hold out much longer without assistance. Had I succeeded in taking Manchester, all would have been well; but now the prospect is, indeed, dark."

"I will explain all to his highness," said Standish; "and should I obtain an interview of the king, I will tell his majesty exactly how your lordship is circumstanced."

"You are a trusty messenger," said the earl. "I need not tell you to lose no time on the journey. Take half a dozen men with you. You had better not set out till night."

Promising to obey his lordship's direction, Standish went to choose the men, and as he proceeded to the stables, he met Gertrude.

"Let me be one of your attendants," she said.

"You!" he exclaimed.

"Yes. I have still my costume as a cavalier," she replied.

"But you forget the distance," he rejoined. "You could not ride from this place to Oxford."

"I think I could," she cried. "But I do not desire to go further than Wigan. Get me through the gates, and across the drawbridge, and I will soon find my way to my father."

"I see your purpose," he replied, "and will aid you. You shall pass out with me to-night. A horse and all equipments shall be found you."

III.

HOW GERTRUDE ACCOMPANIED STANDISH.

Having made all necessary arrangements, Standish returned to the court-yard, where he found Engracia and her attendant Maria.

"I am sorry we shall soon lose you again," she said. "I hear you are starting on another expedition to-night. How long shall you be absent?"

"I can scarcely tell," he replied; "but I suppose three or four days. Should I not return, I hope you will think of me."

"Do not trifle with me," she rejoined, with emotion. "I shall never cease to think of you. But when you *do* return, I hope you will stay here."

"I know not," he replied. "I must obey orders. But unless shut up, I shall not stay here long. When I return from my mission I shall be posted with my lord at Warrington."

"Is Warrington far from this castle?" she inquired.

"Not much more than an hour's ride. If the rebels will let me, I shall often come and see you."

"You must not expose yourself to risk on my account," she said, tenderly. "But pray inform me of your return. The time will pass wearily till then."

"That it will, I am sure, señorita," remarked Maria. "Ah, señor, my young lady thinks only of you."

"Fie, Maria!" cried her mistress. "You should not betray secrets."

"But it is right the caballero should know how much you care for him," said Maria. "It will console him."

"You are right," cried Standish.

In such discourse as this they passed away the time, and so engrossed were they by each other, that they were quite unaware they were watched by the jealous Gertrude.

In obedience to the earl's injunctions, Standish did not prepare to start on his perilous journey till it became dark.

He had already chosen five attendants, but it was not till the last moment that the sixth made his appearance.

The youth had a slight figure, and scarcely looked equal to the journey, but was well mounted.

Standish had taken leave of the earl and countess, so that no delay occurred. The gate was thrown open, the drawbridge lowered, and Standish rode forth with his attendants, and took his way along a lane leading to Skelmersdale.

Thence they galloped across Holland Moor to Pemberton, which was nothing more than a small collection of cottages and an old hall.

From this place a narrow lane brought them to a high road, when Standish came to a halt, and said in a low tone to the youthful attendant we have mentioned:

"This is your road to Wigan. It is not much more than a mile off. Adieu!"

Without waiting for a reply he dashed off on the right, followed by his other attendants.

IV.

HOW GERTRUDE FOUND HER FATHER AT WIGAN.

The youth remained stationary for a moment, and then rousing himself, took the course indicated by his leader.

Very shortly he came in sight of a large town, which, even in the gloom, he could see was surrounded by partly-demolished fortifications.

Presently he was challenged by an advanced guard stationed in front of the gate.

"Who are you?" demanded a hoarse voice.

"A friend," was the reply.

"Are you alone?" demanded the guard.

"Yes—alone."

Two musketeers then stepped forward to reconnoitre the stranger, and the foremost inquired:

"What is your business here at this hour?"

"I desire to see Colonel Rosworm," replied the youth. "I pray you take me to him."

"It is too late," replied the musketeer, gruffly. "You cannot enter the town. Go your way. Return to-morrow morning if you list."

"It is important that I should see Colonel Rosworm to-night. Will you take a message from me to him?"

"No," was the stern answer. "He has

retired to rest, and I will not disturb him."

"He is yonder. I hear his voice."

And the youth called out a few words in German which evidently reached Rosworm's quick ears, for he hastened to the spot.

The musketeers could not understand what passed between Rosworm and the stranger, for their discourse was conducted in a language unknown to them; but they were surprised when the great German engineer took the new comer's horse by the bridle, and led him through the gate into the town, saying to the guard, "It is all right."

In this manner they proceeded along the main street till they came to a large house, at the entrance of which sentinels were placed. Here they stopped.

The youth dismounted, and giving his

horse to one of the sentinels, followed his conductor into the house.

Several Roundhead soldiers made their appearance in the passage, but retired on a word from Rosworm, who ushered the stranger into a large room, dimly lighted by a lamp, where they were quite alone.

No sooner was the door closed, than the engineer affectionately embraced his daughter.

"I ought to chide thee severely for thy conduct," he said, in a voice in which anger struggled with tenderness; "but I cannot do it. I thought thou hadst left me for ever."

"Not so, dear father," she rejoined. "I am always ready to return to you, but I cannot endure these rebels."

"Then why come here, where thou art in the midst of them?" he asked.

"Because I have something important to say to you," she rejoined. "Are you content with the mischief you have done to this town?"

"What mean'st thou?" he said. "I shall not be content till I have fulfilled my engagement. I have undertaken to deliver all the towns in Lancashire to the Parliament."

"I feared as much, dear father," she rejoined. "But I hope to dissuade you from your cruel purpose."

"Thou wilt fail," he said.

"I trust not. You will listen to what I have to say?"

"Humph!" he exclaimed. "It is mere waste of time. I will promise not to assist in any attack on Lathom House—but Warrington is different."

"I hope you will not be able to take the place," she cried.

"Indulge no such notion," he rejoined. "Wigan was more strongly fortified than any other town in Lancashire, and you see how soon it fell. We shall make short work with Warrington."

"I hope you may be unsuccessful, father," she said. "And if I am permitted I will fight against you."

"You will not have the opportunity of doing so, child," he rejoined. "You will remain here for the present."

"May I not return to Lathom House?"

"Not till after the capture of Warrington," he rejoined, in a decided tone. "You should have thought of this before you came hither."

"Oh, father!" she exclaimed, "I judged you very differently."

"I detain you against my will," he said. "But you compel me to act thus by your indiscretion. Were I to let you go, my motives would be misconstrued."

"If this is your fixed determination, father, I shall try to escape," she cried.

"Act as you think proper," he rejoined. "I will not suffer thee to depart."

"Father," she implored, "I pray you let me go! Do not drive me to some desperate act."

Rosworm could not resist her entreaties.

"I ought not to yield," he said. "But thou hast placed me in a disagreeable dilemma, and perhaps this is the best way out of it. Come, then, I will go with thee to the gate."

Without another word he left the room, and she followed him.

The horse was instantly brought by the guard, and when Gertrude had gained the saddle, Rosworm walked by her side to the gate.

Thus escorted, no question was asked, and no hindrance offered to her departure.

V.

HOW GERTRUDE WARNED THE EARL THAT WARRINGTON WAS IN DANGER.

GERTRUDE had failed in her errand. She had found her father impracticable, but she had ascertained that Warrington was to be attacked on the morrow, and resolved to warn the Earl of Derby that the town was in danger. She hastened back as fast as she could to Lathom, and met with no hindrance on the way.

On arriving at the castle, some explanation was necessary to the guard, but they were quickly satisfied, and admittance was given her.

Her first business was to obtain an audience of the earl. Fortunately, he had not retired to rest, but was engaged in converse with the countess and Doctor Rutter in a small chamber adjoining the great hall.

She had no difficulty in obtaining admittance to him, but some explanation was necessary to account for her appearance in male attire. She concealed nothing from the earl, and told him she had been to Wigan, and detailed all that had passed between her and her father, adding, in conclusion:

"I am certain Warrington will be attacked to-morrow morning, my lord."

"In that case, I must go there to-night," said the earl. "But I shall only take the two regiments I brought with me to-day. The men must get ready instantly. I shall not disturb the garrison here. You have rendered me good service," he added to Gertrude, "and I thank you."

"I am sorry I could not serve you better, my lord," she replied. "But I should like to go with you to Warrington—if I may be permitted."

"I admire your spirit," he replied. "But I must refuse your request."

He then went forth to give orders for the immediate departure of the troops.

Shortly afterwards, the trumpet was sounded in the court-yard, and in reply to the summons the men came forth fully equipped.

Torches were lighted, so that the assemblage could be fully seen. Some of the officers of the garrison at Lathom were anxious to attend his lordship, but were not allowed.

Meanwhile, the earl had taken leave of the countess. Though sorely grieved to part with him, she concealed her distress, and strove to cheer him.

"Grieved as I am to part with you, my dear lord," she said, "I would not have you stay, but would rather urge your departure. Whetever may chance at Warrington, have no fear of this castle. Be sure I will keep it for you."

"I have no doubt of that," he rejoined. "I shall make the best defence I can, but should Warrington fall into the hands of the rebels, and should no assistance be sent by the king, I shall retire to the Isle of Man. Thither you can follow with our children. And now farewell, dear heart, I will not say for ever!"

Tenderly embracing her, he bade adieu

to Doctor Rutter, and went forth into the court-yard, where, as already stated, the two regiments were drawn up.

As soon as he had mounted, trumpets were blown, the gates were thrown wide open, and the earl rode forth at the head of his company.

Passing through a wood on the south of the mansion, and riding as rapidly as was consistent with safety across a wide bleak moor to Rainsford, the earl proceeded through Windle and Haydock to Newton, where he halted for a short time, and ascertained that, as yet, Colonel Assheton had made no movement from Wigan.

There was a small Royalist force at Newton, and having given some directions to its leaders, the earl rode on with his company to Warrington, now not more than five miles distant.

VI.

HOW WARRINGTON WAS ASSAULTED BY COLONEL ASSHETON AND COLONEL HOLLAND.

STRONGLY fortified by mud walls with gates, posts and heavy chains, and numerous outworks in advance, possessing, moreover, a strong garrison, the ancient town of Warrington seemed well able to resist any attack made upon it.

The river Mersey, which flowed past the town, was crossed by a strong stone bridge, built by the first Earl of Derby, upwards of a century and a half previously.

With its walls and battlements, a watch-tower in the centre, and an engine to prevent any passage over it, this ancient bridge constituted a powerful defence.

On the summit of the church tower were placed two small pieces of ordnance, while the church itself was converted into a storehouse for ammunition and powder.

From its well-planned defences, its position on the Mersey, its bridge, and its strong garrison, Warrington was deemed impregnable. The governor, Colonel Edward Norris, who acted for Lord Derby, was an officer of great bravery and unquestionable loyalty, and there were others almost equally distinguished in the garrison.

The Earl of Derby's first business on his arrival was to have an interview with the governor, and having explained the position of affairs, he threw himself on a couch, and sought some repose of which he stood greatly in need.

When he awoke, he learnt from the scouts that the enemy was advancing with the evident intention of investing the town, and attacking it on two sides—the force on the west being led by Colonel Assheton, that on the east by Colonel Holland, with whom was Colonel Rosworm.

On receiving this intelligence, the earl immediately sallied forth at the head of a large troop of horse, and attacked Colonel Assheton near Sankey Bridge, driving him back as far as Burton Wood; and he might have routed the whole force, had not Colonel Holland sent a detachment to Assheton's aid, and Lord Derby was thereupon compelled to return to the town, or his retreat would have been cut off.

Not long afterwards the assault was commenced by Colonel Holland, assisted as we have said by Rosworm, and notwithstanding the vigorous defence made by Colonel Norris, part of the mud walls were taken, and it seemed certain that the enemy would succeed in penetrating into the town.

Upon this, the Earl of Derby, who was riding about on his charger, declared that rather than the enemy should capture the town, he would burn it to the ground.

When Colonel Holland and Rosworm heard of this threat, they laughed at it, and redoubled their efforts to advance. But they were stopped by loud explosions, which proved that several houses had been blown up, and flames were soon afterwards perceived bursting forth in different quarters.

The earl had executed his threat.

All the habitations nearest them were on fire, and the conflagration, aided by combustibles, was rapidly extending along the main street.

Struck with consternation at this spectacle, the assailants paused in their efforts, and considered what should be done.

It was impossible now to advance without exposing themselves to the greatest risk—indeed, to almost certain destruction. Besides, as the town would inevitably be burnt down, little would be left them but the mud walls.

From information which they obtained, they learnt that Lord Derby and Colonel Norris, with a large body of men, had retired to the church, where they were secure from the fire, as well as from attack.

Under these circumstances the assailants judged it their wisest course to retire for the night to Sankey, and wait to see what the morrow would bring forth.

It was a night of terror and surprise.

More than half the town was on fire, but no efforts were made by the inhabitants to extinguish the flames. Most of them had crossed the bridge, and found shelter at Groppenhall, Thelwall, and other villages.

But the besiegers were not allowed to rest at Sankey. At midnight the sentinels were shot, and the Parliamentarians, who had fancied themselves in security, were suddenly roused to arms.

The foe was upon them. A fierce fight ensued that lasted more than two hours, and ended in a complete rout of the Parliamentarians, part of whom returned to Wigan, and the rest to Manchester.

Warrington was thus delivered from the rebels, and though the town suffered as much as it would have done had it been ravaged by the enemy—perhaps more—not a murmur was heard from the loyal inhabitants. Every assistance in his power was rendered them by the earl, and in the course of a few days many partly consumed dwellings were again rendered habitable.

As some fears were entertained that another attack on the place would be made by Colonel Assheton from Wigan, Lord Derby remained to protect it.

VII.

HOW STANDISH RETURNED FROM HIS MISSION.

It had now become quite evident to the earl that unless he received prompt and efficient assistance from the king, it would be impossible to continue the struggle. He looked anxiously for Standish's return, but nearly a week elapsed and no tidings were heard of him.

One evening the earl had mounted the watch-tower on the bridge, and was gazing at the river flowing through the narrow arches, when his attention was aroused by the sound of horses' feet, and he saw a Cavalier advancing rapidly along the Chester road, followed by some half-dozen attendants.

Could it be Standish? He watched the new-comer anxiously, and felt convinced he was right in the supposition. Quitting the watch-tower, he hastened towards the gate by which the new-comers would have to enter the town, but long before he reached it, Standish had obtained admittance.

On descrying the earl, the young man flung himself from his steed, and giving the bridle to one of his followers, hurried forward. Lord Derby instantly perceived from his looks that he brought bad news, and inquired:

"Have you seen Prince Rupert?"

"I have, my lord," replied Standish; "and I bring a letter from his highness to my noble lady the countess."

"Is it favourable?" cried the earl. "Will the prince come to us?—will he bring, or send assistance?"

"He cannot, my lord," replied Standish. "The king will not allow him. I represented your lordship's position exactly to his highness, and he sees your peril; but he cannot help you."

"Then all is lost!" cried the earl, in a voice of anguish. "All the sacrifices I have made are useless. You see that this town has been burnt. It was destroyed to save it from the rebels; but it will now fall into their hands."

"I trust not, my lord," said Standish. "I have a message for you from the prince."

"What says he?" cried the earl.

"He counsels your lordship to retire to the Isle of Man, and remain there till better days arrive."

"He is right," said the earl. "I shall

find a safe refuge there. Come with me to Colonel Norris."

Proceeding to a large house near the bridge, they found the governor of the town.

"Captain Standish has just returned from Oxford, and brings me bad news," said the earl. "There is no hope of assistance."

"Then it will be useless to hold out," observed the governor.

"Quite useless," rejoined the earl. "Hoist the white flag, and make the best terms you can with the enemy. My own intention is to retire to the Isle of Man, and there abide my time. To-night I shall go to Lathom, and bid farewell to the countess."

"Will you not take her ladyship with you to Castle Rushen?" asked Colonel Norris.

"She would refuse to accompany me," replied the earl. "But I have no fear for her safety. She has a strong castle, and a strong garrison, and can defend herself. Ride on to Lathom, Frank," he added to Standish, "and deliver Prince Rupert's letter to the countess. Tell her that Warrington must be surrendered. Acquaint her with my resolve, and say I will be with her before midnight to bid her farewell."

"I will, my lord," replied Standish.

As the earl evidently wished to confer with the governor, Standish left them together.

The young man remained for an hour at Warrington to rest his horses and men, and then, after receiving the earl's final commands, set out for Lathom, where he arrived in safety, and delivered the missive to the countess, informing her at the same time that Warrington was about to be surrendered by the governor.

Whatever the countess felt on perusing Prince Rupert's letter, and however distressed she might be by the tidings brought her, and her lord's determination to return to the Isle of Man, she said nothing at the time, but withdrew to her own chamber.

When she had quite regained her composure, she sent for Doctor Rutter, and passed some time in consultation with him.

After this, attended by the chaplain and Standish, she inspected the garrison, examined the stores, and made it understood by all the officers that they must prepare for a siege. They all displayed the utmost zeal.

VIII.

HOW THE EARL TOOK HIS DEPARTURE FOR THE ISLE OF MAN.

Midnight came, but the earl had not arrived, and the countess began to feel some little uneasiness, and this greatly increased when another hour had passed by.

Suddenly, Standish entered to announce that her lord had arrived, and the next moment the earl made his appearance, and clasped her to his breast.

"I have come to bid you adieu!" he said, regarding her tenderly. "Do you approve of my resolution?"

"Entirely," she replied, firmly. "Since assistance has been refused you by the king, you have no alternative. Doctor Rutter, with whom I have conferred, is of the same opinion."

"Since Warrington has fallen, it is useless to continue the struggle at this moment," said the chaplain. "Therefore you will be best away."

"But am I justified in leaving you here?" said the earl to the countess.

"My lord," she replied firmly, "unless you command me to accompany you I will not stir. Let me remain here. I will keep this castle for you against all the combined forces of your enemies. But perhaps they may not attack me."

"Expect no consideration from them," he rejoined, bitterly. "But I will not thwart you. I commit this castle to your charge."

"And I will keep it for you, my lord," replied the courageous lady, in a tone that electrified her hearers. "I will never yield it, but with life. You may rely on me."

"I know it," he replied, with admiration. "You will remain with her ladyship, Rutter?"

"To the last," he replied. "I consider it my duty to stay with her, since she may need counsel and consolation. But there is not a single person in the garrison who will quit her ladyship."

"I think not," said the countess proudly.

"How say you, Frank?" remarked the earl to Standish. "Will you remain here, or accompany me to the Isle of Man?"

"Since your lordship allows me the choice, I will stay here," replied Standish.

"I felt sure you would so decide," said the earl. "You shall attend me to Whitehaven, where I shall embark, and then return. Go and prepare, I shall not tarry long here."

On this, Standish quitted the room, and Doctor Rutter was about to follow, but the earl stopped him.

"Do not go, Rutter" he remarked. "I have nothing to say in private to her ladyship."

"Will you not see your children ere you depart, my lord?" said the countess. "They have not retired to rest, and will be sadly grieved indeed if they do not embrace you."

"Nay, then, bring them to me at once," he cried.

Summoned by Rutter, the three noble damsels rushed into the room, and were tenderly embraced by their father, who blessed them as he strained them to his breast.

"You will soon come back to us, dear

father, will you not?" they cried in concert.

"I hope so," he rejoined. "If not you must come to me. I am going to Castle Rushen."

"We would rather remain at Lathom,' they exclaimed.

"Ay, it is best you should stay with your mother," he rejoined. "And now adieu, my darlings. If I remain here a moment longer I shall never be able to tear myself away."

Again embracing them all—again clasping the countess to his breast, he hastily quitted the room.

In the court-yard he found the escort he had brought with him consisting of a dozen well-armed and well mounted troopers— not more. All the officers of the garrison were assembled.

"Farewell, gentlemen," he cried, as he

sprang into the saddle. "I commit the countess and my children to your care."

"We will guard them with our lives," they rejoined with one voice.

Attended by Standish, and followed by the troopers, the earl then rode through the gateway.

His heart was very sorrowful, and he said to himself:

"Shall I ever return here? Shall I ever behold these dear ones again?"

End of Book the Fourth.

Book the Fifth.

THE BELEAGUERED MANSION.

I.

OF THE GARRISON AT LATHOM HOUSE.

NEARLY two months had elapsed since the Earl of Derby's departure to the Isle of Man, where he had been occupied in repressing a threatened insurrection and re-establishing his authority, and though Warrington had surrendered, and almost every castle, or fortified mansion in the county was now in the hands of the Parliamentary leaders, no attack had as yet been made on Lathom House.

Its real strength not being known, it was thought the castle could be easily taken at any time. Though the countess had not been disturbed, she was virtually a prisoner in her own house, and never stirred forth without a guard. She made no display whatever, but was always secretly increasing the strength of the garrison. In fact, the castle, which was a small town in itself, was in a perfect state of defence, and quite capable of standing a lengthened siege.

Immediately after the surrender of Warrington, a summons was sent by Colonel Holland, the Governor of Manchester, to the countess, requiring her to acknowledge the Parliament, or deliver up her mansion, but to this demand she returned a haughty and peremptory refusal.

"Take back this message to the Governor of Manchester," she said. "I will do nothing derogatory to my husband's honour.

I will neither acknowledge the Parliament —nor give up my house. But I promise to attack no one — and only to defend myself. All I desire is to remain here peaceably, and I trust I shall not be disturbed."

This response seemed reasonable to Colonel Holland, and for a time she continued unmolested.

Not desiring to give the enemy a pretext for assailing her, the countess carefully restrained her garrison from giving them any provocation, and forbade them to plunder any houses belonging to Parliamentarians, or commit any outrage whatever. They might defend themselves, but must not make reprisals.

By this judicious conduct she remained free from attack, and was enabled to strengthen herself, and add to her stores.

At this time the number of the garrison

was fully three hundred men, many of whom were expert marksmen, several having been the earl's keepers and fowlers. The majority were armed with muskets, but some carried long fowling-pieces and screwed guns.

Sixteen of the best marksmen kept watch on every alternate night, while an equal number of musketeers occupied the towers during the day, in addition to the engineers who had charge of the cannon.

Besides Standish, there were five officers, whom we have already particularised, but it may be proper to call over the roll again.

All were men of good family: Henry Ogle of Prescot—Edward Chisenhale of Chisenhale, near Chorley—William Farmer, a Scottish gentleman who had served in the Low Countries—Edward Rawsthorne of New Hall—Molineux Radcliffe, a relative of the Radcliffes of Ordsall—and John Foxe of Rhodes.

There were likewise six lieutenants—namely, Bretergh, Penketh, Walthew, Worrall, Kay, and Halsall.

Chief in command was William Farrington of Worden, appointed major of the garrison by the countess. He had suffered much for his attachment to Lord Derby and loyalty to the king. He had been a colonel of militia, and a commissioner of array, but his goods were seized and his property sequestered by the Parliament. Major Farrington was a man of excellent judgment, and the countess had entire reliance upon him, and consulted him on all occasions.

Lady Derby had now three chaplains in the house. Archdeacon Rutter, with whom the reader is already acquainted, Doctor Brideoake, and the Reverend John

Lake. Service was always performed twice a day in the chapel, and on special occasions more frequently. Within the stronghold the greatest order and discipline prevailed. Not one person had been punished for disobedience or neglect of duty.

Already, we have endeavoured to familiarise the reader with the appearance of this proud embattled mansion, with its wide courts, its circuit of walls, its great gate-towers, its broad moat, strengthened by stout palisades on either bank, and, above all, its lofty central tower. But we must again refer to the picture, in order to notice a marked change that had taken place in its appearance.

Though more strongly garrisoned than formerly, Lathom looked less menacing. In each tower on the walls were six pieces of ordnance. But neither engineers nor musketeers were visible. They were there, but did not show themselves. Only on the gate-towers could the guard be distinguished. No banner floated as of yore from the summit of the Eagle Tower, and the sentinels seemed to have been removed.

But these appearances were deceptive. Strict watch was kept night and day on tower and rampart, and on every part of the castle.

That officers and men found this inactive life wearisome is certain. They would have preferred annoying the enemy by an occasional sortie, but Major Farrington, acting upon the countess's instructions, would not permit them. She was resolved not to provoke assault. It surprised her that the enemy allowed her to remain quiet so long, but she would not precipitate matters.

II.

HOW CAPTAIN MARKLAND BROUGHT A LETTER FROM SIR THOMAS FAIRFAX TO THE COUNTESS.

At length an event occurred that brought about the attack the countess had been so studious to avoid.

Her chief enemy was Colonel Alexander Rigby, an active Parliamentary officer, who harboured a strong vindictive feeling against the Earl of Derby, and now sought to gratify it.

The traitor Bootle, who had only been severely wounded in his attempt to capture the queen, and had since joined Rigby, was sent by him to plunder the countess's tenants and neighbours, and arrest all who attempted to take refuge in the castle.

Hitherto, Don Fortunio and his daughter had been allowed to remain without molestation at Knowsley, whither they had removed about a month ago, but now they were taken prisoners by Bootle, who intended to carry them off to Wigan, but was prevented. Having learnt his design Standish attacked him with a small party of horse, rescued the captives, and conveyed them safely to Lathom.

In this skirmish, several of Bootle's men were wounded. Deeply resenting the affront, as he conceived it, Colonel Rigby immediately represented the matter to Sir Thomas Fairfax, general of the Parliamentary forces in Lancashire, who was then in Manchester.

Reluctant to disturb the countess, Fairfax at length yielded to Rigby's importunities, and called a council of war, at which Colonel Holland, the Governor of Manchester, Colonel Assheton of Middleton, Colonel Moore of Bank Hall, and Rigby himself were present.

After some discussion, it was resolved that a strong force should be sent against Lathom, and the countess summoned to surrender.

Immediate warning of their design was given to the countess, who had a spy among the enemy, and she was enabled to prepare for them. The three Parliamentary leaders, however, gave out that they were about to march to Bolton and Wigan, and thence to Westmoreland, but her ladyship was not surprised to find they had fixed their quarters at various points round the hall.

Next day, Captain Markland, the Parliamentary general's aide-de-camp, attended by a small guard, presented himself at the gate of Lathom House and desired admittance, stating that he had a letter for her ladyship from Sir Thomas Fairfax.

This being reported to the countess, she gave orders that the messenger should be admitted, but his attendants must remain outside.

The gate was then opened, and Captain Markland rode into the court-yard, and was shortly afterwards ushered by Major Farrington into the presence of the countess.

Captain Markland was tall, strongly built, and well equipped. A morion with a ridge on the top, a gorget, cuirass, and taches met by immense gambado boots, formed his accoutrements, and he had a large cutting sword by his side.

On approaching the countess, he made her a military salute, which she haughtily returned.

"You come from Sir Thomas Fairfax, as I understand, sir," she remarked.

"I am the bearer of a despatch from the general to your ladyship," he replied.

Taking a letter from his belt, he gave it to Major Farrington, who handed it to the countess.

Calmly and without any change of countenance, Lady Derby read the letter, and then said to the messenger:

"I presume you are aware of the purport of this missive?"

Captain Markland replied in the affirmative.

"It is a requisition from Sir Thomas Fairfax," he said, "enjoining your ladyship to yield up Lathom House on such honourable conditions as he shall propose."

"Does Sir Thomas Fairfax require immediate compliance with his injunction?" she asked.

"Even so, madam," replied Markland. "And I trust I may be able to carry him back an answer to that effect."

"You are in a strange hurry, sir," remarked the countess. "Think you I can decide at once upon a matter of such import. My lord has left me in charge of this mansion, and I cannot yield it up without due consideration. I require a week's delay."

"I am not prepared to say the delay will be granted, madam," replied Markland, "but I will deliver your answer to the general. Do you hold out any promise of compliance at the expiration of that time?"

"I hold out nothing," replied the countess. "Put any construction you deem proper on my words. I shall consult with my advisers," she added, glancing at Major Farrington and her three chaplains who were standing near.

"I trust they will counsel you to submit to necessity, madam," observed Markland.

Major Farrington would have spoken, but the countess checked him by a look and said haughtily to the messenger:

"Take back my answer, sir."

Upon this, Captain Markland bowed and retired, and was conducted to the courtyard by Standish.

As he mounted his steed, the Parliamentary officer remarked:

"We shall soon be masters here."

"Not so soon," rejoined Standish, contemptuously.

III.

HOW CAPTAIN MARKLAND BROUGHT A SECOND LETTER FROM SIR THOMAS FAIRFAX, AND IN WHAT MANNER THE COUNTESS REPLIED TO IT.

AFTER this visit, the countess was allowed to remain in peace for a few days, but from the summit of the lofty Eagle Tower she perceived that her enemies were increasing in number, and drawing the cordon of troops still more tightly around her.

Colonel Assheton was stationed at Burscough Priory and Blyth Hall — Colonel Moore was near Cross Hall—and Colonel Rigby at Newburgh.

As to Sir Thomas Fairfax, she learnt from her scouts that he had taken up his quarters at Knowsley.

During this interval, she restrained her soldiers from making an attack on the enemy.

Hitherto, fresh provisions had been regularly brought by her tenants, but now these were almost entirely cut off, and the countess was most unwilling to have recourse to her stores. Parties of the enemy were constantly on the watch to cut off supplies.

The utmost enthusiasm prevailed in the garrison; officers and men were in excellent spirits. The heroic countess had inspired them all with an ardour and zeal akin to her own, and they longed for an opportunity of distinguishing themselves. As we have said, the utmost regularity was observed. The men were daily inspected by Major

Farrington, accompanied by Standish or some other officer, and no one was ever found absent from his post. The horses were regularly exercised in the court-yard, and thereby kept in health and good condition. Nothing, in short, was neglected.

The routine of the countess's life was exactly the same that it had been. Twice in each day, sometimes thrice, service was performed in the chapel by Archdeacon Rutter, Doctor Brideoake, or Mr. Lake, and she always attended with her family. All the officers of the garrison, and such of the men as were not actually employed, together with part of the household, likewise attended; and nothing could be more impressive than the service—nothing more striking than the picture presented by the chapel filled with armed men surrounding the noble lady and her daughters. Their deportment was most serious and devout. At these services Gertrude Rosworm was always present.

On the third day after Captain Markland's visit to the countess, another letter was brought her by the same officer from Sir Thomas Fairfax.

In this despatch the Parliamentary general regretted that he could not accord her ladyship the delay she required, but he added, with some courtesy:

"Since nothing can be arranged without a conference, I hope your ladyship will come in your coach to Knowsley, where I and my three colonels will meet you, to discuss the terms of surrender. You need have no apprehension. I guarantee your personal safety."

The countess read this letter with great indignation.

"In sending this message," she said,

scornfully, "Sir Thomas Fairfax has forgotten what is due to my lord and to myself. I decline to meet him and his colonels at Knowsley. If they desire to confer with me they must come here. It is meet they should wait on me, not I on them."

"I will deliver your ladyship's message," replied Captain Markland.

Later on in the same day he returned, bringing another letter from General Sir Thomas Fairfax, to say that he did not desire to put her ladyship to inconvenience, and would, therefore, wait upon her next day, at Lathom House.

IV.

HOW SIR THOMAS FAIRFAX CAME TO LATHOM HOUSE, AND WHAT PASSED BETWEEN HIM AND THE COUNTESS.

NEXT day, about noon, in accordance with the message he had sent, Sir Thomas Fairfax, attended by a troop of horse, arrived at Lathom House.

Leaving his guard at a short distance from the castle, he rode up to the gateway, accompanied only by Captain Markland, thus showing the perfect reliance he had on the countess's honour.

The distinguished Parliamentary general

was then about thirty-three, but looked, perhaps, a little older. Tall, and well-proportioned, he had handsome, but strongly-marked features, characterised by a grave and sombre expression. He had more the air and manner of a Cavalier than a Roundhead; but he had no sympathies whatever with the Royalist cause.

Though of noble birth on both sides, being the son of Lord Fairfax by Mary, daughter of the Earl of Mulgrave, Sir Thomas preferred a democratic form of government, and hated the Court. Having served in Holland under Lord Vere, he was a thorough soldier. He was likewise highly accomplished, and though not learned, well read.

Already he had played an important part in the Civil Wars, and at the period in question promised to become the foremost man in the Parliamentary party, though he was subsequently overshadowed by the bold and crafty Cromwell.

Sir Thomas Fairfax's accoutrements were a steel cuirass, with cuisses, and buff boots, and his sword was sustained by a richly ornamented baldrick. Instead of a steel head-piece, however, he wore a broad-leaved hat with a black feather.

As Sir Thomas Fairfax rode up to the mansion he was quite surprised at the formidable appearance it presented. Suddenly it had become a fortress, and a very strong one. Hitherto, as we have shown, it had been the policy of the countess to conceal her defensive preparations from the enemy, but she now ostentatiously displayed them. The aspect of the place was altogether changed. It looked threatening and defiant. A broad banner floated from the summit of the Eagle Tower, bearing the proud motto of the Stanleys—SANS CHANGER. The large pieces of ordnance on the high turreted gateway, and in the numerous towers on the ramparts, were unmasked. The engineers were at their posts, and the walls were thronged with musketeers.

Scanning the place with a curious eye, Fairfax saw the strength of its position, and how well it was garrisoned.

But another surprise awaited him.

When the drawbridge was lowered, and the gates were thrown open to admit him and his aide-de-camp, an imposing spectacle was presented.

Two hundred stalwart musketeers, fully armed and equipped, and having their lieutenants with them, were ranged in double lines, extending from the gate to the doorway of the mansion.

On his entrance into the court, Fairfax was received by Major Farrington and Captains Standish and Chisenhale, all three fully accoutred, and as soon as he had dismounted, he was conducted by the major along the living avenue we have described to the entrance.

As he marched along, the musketeers were struck by his looks and martial bearing, but they allowed no admiration to appear, and regarded him sternly.

Very few words passed between the Parliamentary general and his conductor, but they were courteous towards each other. More musketeers were on the steps, and the doorway was environed by officers of the household.

Ceremoniously conducted to the presence-chamber, Fairfax perceived the countess at the upper end, seated like a queen on a high chair, with her daughters beside her. Near her were her three chaplains, and Captains Rawsthorne and Molineux Radcliffe were in attendance.

"The countess keeps a court, I perceive, at Lathom," observed Sir Thomas Fairfax to Major Farrington. "I did not expect to be treated with so much ceremony."

"Her ladyship desires to do you honour, general," rejoined the other.

As Sir Thomas approached, the countess arose, and received him with stately courtesy, praying him to be seated.

"You are welcome to Lathom, Sir Thomas," she said, "albeit you come as an enemy."

"I thank your ladyship for your welcome," he rejoined. "You have surprised me. I own I did not expect to find you so well prepared."

"Doubtless you expected to find me ready to submit, Sir Thomas," she said, with a haughty smile; "but such is not my intention."

"Resistance to the forces I can bring will

be useless, madam," he remarked. "I hope, therefore, your ladyship will listen to the conditions I have to propose."

"Let me hear them," she rejoined.

"From the display I have just seen, I find your ladyship has a large stock of arms, and I doubt not abundance of ammunition. These stores must be delivered up to me."

At this demand the countess's attendants exchanged glances. She answered calmly but firmly:

"When I procured the arms you have just seen, Sir Thomas, and such munitions of war as I possess, it was to defend myself against my enemies, and not to attack them. Unless my house had been strongly garrisoned, I should have long since been driven from it. I have been subjected to every kind of provocation and annoyance from the soldiers of the Parliament, but I have not retaliated, and have restrained my own officers and men as much as possible."

"I have heard otherwise, madam," rejoined Fairfax. "I am told that your soldiers have been in the habit of stripping the country round about, and if your garrison is well provisioned, such must have been the case. I am also informed that some of your officers have seized upon several persons well affected to the Parliament, and brought them as prisoners into this stronghold, demanding large sums for their ransom."

"Whoever said so has belied me," remarked the countess.

"I can give a positive denial to that statement, Sir Thomas," interposed Major Farrington. "No such thing has occurred."

"It is an invention of the false traitor

Bootle," remarked the countess. "My soldiers are not marauders."

"I will not dispute the point, madam," said Fairfax. "I repeat that the arms and ammunition in this fortress—for such it is—must be delivered up to me. On your compliance with this condition, I engage that your ladyship and all your family and household, with all officers, soldiers, and others, composing your garrison shall be suffered to depart to Chester, or any other town they may select in that county—but not in Lancashire."

"I will answer for the whole garrison, Sir Thomas," observed Major Farrington. "Unless by her ladyship's commands—not an officer—not a man will depart."

"And we, her ladyship's chaplains," added Archdeacon Rutter, "refuse to leave her unless in obedience to her injunctions."

"And such injunctions I shall never give," said the countess.

"Neither your chaplains nor any of your household are required to leave you, madam," said Fairfax. "They will be allowed to reside with you at Knowsley, which will be placed at your ladyship's disposal on your submission to the Parliment."

At this proposition all the countess's pride was aroused, and she said haughtily and indignantly:

"And think you, Sir Thomas, that I would act disloyally to my sovereign, and undutifully to my lord and husband, to obtain any favour from the Parliament? No! I reject the offer—scornfully reject it."

"Have patience, madam, and hear me to an end," said Fairfax. "If you prefer it, you shall be allowed to rejoin the earl, your husband, in the Isle of Man, and take with you your family and household."

"Hear me, Sir Thomas," cried the countess. "Much as I desire to behold my lord and husband again—greatly as I suffer at my prolonged separation from him—I will not swerve for a moment, even in thought, from my duty. Unless my lord himself commands me, I will never leave Lathom House. I will rather perish than relinquish my charge."

"Consideration for others may move you, madam," remarked Fairfax. "Your daughters, I doubt not, would fain be with their father."

"You are mistaken, Sir Thomas," said the Lady Henriette Marie, with great spirit. "We will never leave our dear mother, the countess."

"Never!" cried the two others with equal spirit. "We will perish with her."

"You hear, Sir Thomas," said the countess with a proud smile. "We are all of the same opinion."

"So I find, madam," replied Fairfax, "and I much fear I may be compelled to have recourse to extremities, which I am most anxious to avoid. However, in the hope that you may yet change your mind. I will give you two more days for reflection, and during that interval I shall be willing to receive any proposition you may think fit to make to me. You have able advisers with you," he added, glancing at Major Farrington and the three divines, and will do well to profit by their counsel."

"I should counsel nothing that the Earl of Derby himself would not approve," observed Major Farrington. "And I am certain he would never advise a surrender."

The interview then terminated.

Bowing to the countess, who arose and

returned the salutation, Sir Thomas Fairfax departed. He was attended by Major Farrington and Standish, and as he passed through the lines of musketeers, who were still stationed in the court-yard, there arose from them a loud shout, which was taken up by their comrades on the towers and ramparts.

"God save the Earl of Derby and the king," resounded on all sides.

V.

HOW A STAND IN THE PARK WAS DESTROYED BY RIGBY, AND A MILL BURNT.

Fairfax rode back in a very thoughtful mood to Ormskirk, where he found Colonel Rigby, and told him his errand had been unsuccessful.

"I expected nothing else from that impracticable and imperious dame," said Rigby. "Then the siege will commence at once?"

"No; I have given her a further delay of two days," replied Fairfax.

"I am sorry for it," said Rigby. "Nothing will be gained by the delay."

"Perhaps reflection may induce her to submit, and I do not wish to treat her harshly," observed Fairfax. "On the day after to-morrow, should I not hear from her in the interim, Colonel Morgan shall take a final message. Meantime, some slight work may be done. Within the park, at the south of the mansion, is a stand from which the earl used to shoot deer. Of late, it appears, this stand has been used as a receptacle for provisions—carcases of sheep and oxen — which have been secretly conveyed to the mansion. It must be destroyed."

"It shall be," said Rigby.

"There is also a windmill on the road to Newburgh, which I make no doubt the countess has found useful. No more corn must be ground there."

"I will take care of that," rejoined Rigby, with a laugh.

"My object is to cut off all supplies," observed Fairfax; "and I believe the loss of that storehouse in the park, together with the windmill, will seriously inconvenience the garrison."

"I doubt it not," said Rigby. "Shall I instruct Captain Browne, the engineer, to draw the lines round the mansion?"

"Ay, that may be done, to show we are in earnest," said Fairfax. "But no attack must be made till the siege is declared."

Rigby immediately proceeded with a troop of horse to the stand in the south park. Three or four persons were within it, but they fled on the approach of the Parliamentarians, leaving behind them a large stock of meat and provisions.

After the structure had been demolished, Rigby took his men to the windmill. The place was unguarded, and no one was to be seen but the miller, who resolutely refused them admittance, and drew up the ladder, so that they could not reach the door, which was high up in the building. At the same time, he himself disappeared.

With some difficulty the ladder was got down, and a couple of troopers mounted it, but the foremost stopped at the door, for he discovered that the interior of the mill was on fire, and turning round, communicated this disagreeable information to his leader.

"Heed not the fire," cried Rigby. "Go in and extinguish it."

"It cannot be extinguished," replied the man. "It burns furiously. I dare not enter."

"What has become of the miller?" shouted Rigby.

"I see him not," replied the trooper. "But most assuredly he will perish in the flames if he comes not forth instantly."

"Look in once more, and tell me if there is much corn in the mill," said Rigby.

The man did as he was bidden, but quickly drew back his head, and dashing down the ladder, upset his comrades on the lower steps.

In another moment the flames burst from the door and window.

As soon as the man had recovered speech, Rigby again put the question to him:

"Didst thou see much corn in the mill?"

"Yea, verily," replied the man. "It seemed to me filled with corn."

"Then let it burn," cried Rigby, "and the miller with it."

And without making an effort to save anything, he rode off, followed by his men.

VI.

WHAT HAPPENED IN THE RUINS OF BURSCOUGH PRIORY.

BETWEEN Lathom House and Ormskirk, in the midst of a wood, stood Burscough Priory — a large religious establishment that had been suffered to go to decay. But the ruins were very picturesque and beautiful, and contained many sculptured shrines and other monuments.

Rigby had heard of the priory, but had not seen it, and he now determined to inspect the ruins.

Taking with him half a dozen men, he sent the rest of his troops to Ormskirk, and rode through the wood to Burscough.

Resolved to examine the interior of the priory, he dismounted, and giving his horse to one of the troopers, he entered the ruins, but had not advanced far, when, to his surprise, he saw a grave-looking personage advancing towards him, who saluted him courteously.

A moment's reflection convinced Rigby that this must be the Spanish gentleman who had been staying at Knowsley, and he therefore said to him sternly:

"If I mistake not, you are Don Fortunio Alava?"

The stranger replied in the affirmative, and added by way of explanation, though he could scarcely make himself understood, since he spoke English with difficulty:

"I have come hither with my daughter.

She is praying at a shrine yonder. You will not disturb her?"

"This praying at shrines, and worshipping of images, is an abomination to me," rejoined Rigby."

" But here—in this retired place—such prayers can offend no one," protested Don Fortunio.

"They offend me," said Rigby. "Doubtless you have come here from Lathom House?"

Don Fortunio replied in the affimative.

"Then return thither forthwith," said Rigby. "It is well for you that there is a truce with the countess, or I had made you a prisoner."

"You are mistaken, Colonel Rigby," said Standish, suddenly appearing from behind a monument, which had hitherto concealed him. " Don Fortunio Alava and his daughter are not unprotected."

"They should have kept within Lathom House at this time," said Rigby. "If they give my soldiers provocation I cannot be answerable for the consequences."

"What provocation can they give your men?" demanded Standish.

"It is an offence to them that Papists should come here to pray," said Rigby; "and they will not permit it. The Spaniards had best go back to Lathom House."

"They are returning to Knowsley, whence they were forcibly taken by Captain Bootle," said Standish.

"That cannot be permitted," rejoined Rigby.

"You will not dispute this warrant from Sir Thomas Fairfax, colonel," said Standish, taking a paper from his belt. "By it Don Antonio Alava and his daughter, with her attendant, are licensed to reside at Knowsley Hall."

" Let me look at the warrant," said Rigby.

After glancing at it he said, sternly:

" I am satisfied. You are at liberty to conduct them to Knowsley—but you yourself must return to Lathom."

" Such is my intention," replied Standish.

Upon this Rigby departed, and mounting his horse rode off with his men.

As soon as he was gone, Engracia and Maria made their appearance from another part of the ruins.

" Heaven be praised that dreadful man is gone!" cried Engracia. " I was afraid we should be made prisoners."

" I have got a safe-conduct for you from the general," replied Standish; " and even the audacious Rigby would not dare to disobey it. You can now return to Knowsley."

"But I shall be afraid to remain there," she said.

"You will be safer there than at Lathom," said Standish.

"But you will never be able to come to Knowsley when the siege commences?" she remarked.

"Not often, I fear," he replied. "All communication will be cut off by the enemy's lines."

"Then I will stay at Lathom."

"But the countess may not desire to have us there," observed her father. "We must not presume too far on her hospitality."

"Let us see her once more, dear father, before we return to Knowsley?" said Engracia.

"She must not be put to the slightest inconvenience. I will never consent to that," said Don Fortunio.

The horsemen whom Standish had brought with him, and Don Fortunio's steed, and the two palfreys belonging to Engracia and her attendant, were in waiting at the back of the ruins, and so well concealed, that they had escaped the notice of Rigby and his troopers.

On the arrival of the party at Lathom, the countess chanced to be in the courtyard, and without a moment's hesitation declared that, under the circumstances, they ought to proceed to Knowsley.

"With Sir Thomas Fairfax's warrant you will be quite safe there," she said, "and will have none of the inconvenience you would have to endure here."

Engracia would much rather have remained at Lathom with all its perils, but Don Fortunio was perfectly satisfied, and thanked her ladyship for her consideration. So they set out at once for Knowsley, and were escorted thither by Standish.

VII.

OF THE MESSAGE BROUGHT BY COLONEL MORGAN TO THE COUNTESS.

NEXT day, the countess prepared for the reception of the messenger whom she knew would be sent to her by Sir Thomas Fairfax.

About an hour before noon, Colonel Morgan arrived, attended by a dozen troopers, whom he was obliged to leave outside the gate. No display was made of the strength of the garrison, as was done when Sir Thomas Fairfax visited the castle.

Colonel Morgan dismounted in the outer court, and was at once conducted to the countess.

A man of small stature, with a very fierce expression of countenance, heightened by a pair of piercing black eyes. His manner was exceedingly consequential, far more so than that of Fairfax, and he comported himself very haughtily towards Major Farrington, who received him, and conducted him to the countess.

Colonel Morgan had won a considerable reputation for activity and courage, and was reputed a very skilful engineer. As he marched through the court with Major Farrington, he encountered several of the officers, and eyed them sharply, almost menacingly, and he also glanced inquisitively at the ramparts.

The countess received him in the presence-chamber, but very coldly, being highly displeased by his manner. Only Archdeacon Rutter and Captain Standish were with her at the time.

In a somewhat insolent tone he informed her that Sir Thomas Fairfax agreed to her conditions, and would allow her to take her children, her chaplains, and her servants to the Isle of Man, but she must disband all her men, and prepare to receive an officer and forty Parliamentary soldiers as her guard.

"Disband all my men?" cried the countess.

"Before noon to-morrow," said Colonel Morgan, peremptorily.

"And you, I presume, are the officer in command?" remarked the countess.

"Your ladyship has guessed aright. It is so," he replied. "I trust I shall be able to carry back a satisfactory answer to the general."

"You will tell Sir Thomas Fairfax that I refuse his proposition — entirely refuse it," she rejoined. "And I am heartily glad he has refused mine. Were it to save my life I would not renew the offer. Had my lord been in command here you had not dared to offer this insult to him."

"No insult is intended to your ladyship," remarked Colonel Morgan. "The general merely requires you to disband your garrison."

"Is it not an affront to send such a message to me?" said the countess. "Did Sir Thomas expect compliance? If he did, he little knows me. I am ready to resist his utmost violence, and trust in Heaven for protection and deliverance. As to you, sir, who have dared to bring me this insolent message, and have ventured to intimate to me that you are appointed to the command of the castle—you shall never set foot in it again."

"I may not be admitted, madam, but it is possible I may enter, nevertheless," said Morgan, boldly.

"Shall I cast him forth, madam, for his insolence and presumption?" cried Standish.

"No, I have promised him free access and a safe return," said the countess. "But he has abused his license."

"I do not desire to offend your ladyship, and am sorry if I have done so," said Colonel Morgan, in a slightly apologetic tone. "I share in the high respect which the general bears for you, and regret that you will not submit to the ordinances of the Parliament. Resistance will be impossible against the large force we shall bring, and by which the castle will very shortly be completely invested. We have ordnance of the largest size, bombards, basilisks, and a great mortar, that will cast forth grenades that cannot fail to burn down the place."

"I fear not your grenades," said the countess. "Heaven will protect me."

"Your terrible mortar will do us no mischief," said Standish. "We will take it from you."

"That is not all," said Morgan. "We will proceed against you by sap and mine."

"We will meet you however you may come," said Standish.

"Enough of this," cried the countess. "I make no boast of my strength, but my cause is just, and I am assured it will triumph."

"May I have a word more with your ladyship ere I depart?" said Morgan. "I am authorised by Sir Thomas Fairfax to grant you another day's delay if you desire it."

"I will not be beholden to your general for any further favour," replied the countess. "Let him come how he will, and when he will, he shall find me prepared. Conduct the messenger to the gate."

While mounting his horse in the courtyard, Colonel Morgan said to Standish, who had conducted him thither:

"I am persuaded this is not the last interview I shall have with her ladyship. Possibly, when I am next admitted to her presence, she may treat me with more courtesy than on the present occasion."

"Before that, I trust, you and I shall meet again, colonel," said Standish, significantly.

VIII.

HOW THE INTRENCHMENTS WERE MADE.

By this time the Parliamentarians had taken up their quarters at various points round the castle.

Colonel Rigby was encamped near Newburgh, Colonel Moore on the road to Ormskirk, and Colonel Assheton and Sir Thomas Fairfax on the south side, where the tents could be descried amongst the trees.

The besiegers now numbered a force of more than two thousand men—five hundred horse, and fifteen hundred foot—quite sufficient, it was thought, for the reduction of the place.

The mansion was now completely invested, parties of men being posted so closely together that all communication with friends was cut off.

Already the lines had been marked out by the engineers, and the pioneers had commenced digging the trenches. They were assisted by several hundred sturdy yeomen and hinds, all of them being Lord Derby's tenants or servants, who were forced by threats and blows to do work that was most distasteful to them.

Some of these poor fellows broke away and ran towards the castle, but the mounted guard galloped after them and brought them back.

The intrenchments were begun at night at the distance of a musket-shot from the mansion, and in a place screened by the rising ground from the ordnance on the towers, and the pioneers and their assistants laboured so hard that before dawn considerable progress had been made. Concealment was then no longer possible, and fire was opened upon them from the walls of the castle, but little mischief was done.

From this time the work proceeded rapidly, being continued night and day without intermission. A deep trench, sheltered by a breastwork of earth, gradually encircled the mansion, and imprisoned its occupants. Constant attacks were made on the pioneers, but no real interruption was effected, and the work went on.

Posted on the Eagle Tower, the countess viewed the progress of this work with ill-suppressed rage, but without uneasiness. In this exalted position, she was out of reach of the enemy's guns, for as yet no large piece of ordnance had been directed against the house, and all shot had been fired against the ramparts.

No serious assault, however, had been made; nor did any such seem intended.

Evidently, the design of Sir Thomas Fairfax, and the other Parliamentary leaders, was to terrify the countess into submission, but if they could have seen her on the Eagle Tower, with Major Farrington, Archdeacon Rutter, and her daughters, they would have felt she would not be easily intimidated. Her sole feeling was that of anger against her foes, and an almost irrepressible desire to attack them. But she was far too prudent not to check the impulse.

Not unfrequently, was Gertrude Rosworm present, and if her sentiments could be judged by her flashing eyes, she shared the countess's indignation, and longed to assail the besiegers.

From this eminent position, the beholders not only overlooked the rising ground on the further side of the moat, and the breastwork of the trenches, but could distinguish the pioneers and their assistants at work. They saw the Parliamentary commanders riding from point to point, each with a troop of horse; they saw the numerous parties of infantry posted around; and they likewise descried in the distance the different encampments of the enemy.

While they were gazing at this picture, Sir Thomas Fairfax, whom they easily recognised, rode round the intrenchments, followed by a troop of horse. He was attended by Colonel Browne, the chief engineer, and Colonel Morgan, and halted ever and anon to inspect the works.

Several shots were fired at him, and though he escaped, two of his men were killed. He did not seem in the slightest degree disturbed by these occurrences, but continued his inspection quietly, as if nothing had happened.

The countess could not help admiring his coolness and courage, and she was still watching him as he moved on, when Captain Standish made his appearance.

"I have a request to prefer to your ladyship," he said. "It is that Captain Chisenhale and myself may be permitted to sally forth on the enemy to-morrow morning. The trenches are now nearly opposite the gateway, and we wish to give the pioneers a check. Captain Chisenhale will take with him a hundred musketeers, and I will support him with a dozen horse. Captain Ogle will cover our retreat."

Before making a reply, the countess glanced at Major Farrington who was standing near.

"'Tis too hazardous," he replied. "If twenty or thirty musketeers are left behind in the trenches the loss will be serious to your ladyship."

"But we shall strike a heavy blow against the enemy, and bring back arms and prisoners," said Standish. "As yet we have done nothing. 'Tis time our assailants should be reminded that they have good soldiers to deal with."

"True," remarked the countess. "I consented to the attack. I have perfect reliance on you and Captain Chisenhale."

"We will not disappoint your ladyship," said Standish.

"I hope you are not too sanguine of success," said Major Farrington.

"The first blow is half the battle, and we must strike it," rejoined Standish. "If we are successful—as I believe we shall be—the enemy will be disheartened, and the garrison encouraged. It will gladden Captain Chisenhale to learn that I have obtained your ladyship's assent to the sally."

IX.

OF THE SORTIE MADE BY CAPTAINS CHISENHALE AND STANDISH.

Next morning, at an early hour, as previously arranged, both gates of the castle were thrown open, the drawbridge was lowered, and a hundred stalwart musketeers, headed by Captain Chisenhale and Lieutenant Bretergh, suddenly sallied forth. They were quickly followed by Captain Standish and a dozen well-mounted and well-armed troopers.

As soon as the musketeers and troopers

had crossed the drawbridge, which they did with great expedition, it was instantly raised, and the outer gate shut.

Meanwhile every precaution had been taken. The cannoniers in the two tall towers, flanking the gate-house, were standing beside their guns with lighted matches in their hands, and the large guard-chamber above the gate was filled with musketeers, with whom were Captain Ogle and Lieutenant Kay.

Indeed, the whole garrison was astir, and there were numerous lookers-on at the sortie, though being concealed in the towers on the walls, they could not be descried by the enemy.

Amongst the watchers was the countess herself. Already she had ascended the Eagle Tower—the only persons with her being Archdeacon Rutter and Gertrude Rosworm.

She had seen the brave band of musketeers assemble noiselessly in the court, where they were marshalled by Captain Chisenhale and his lieutenant, who gave them their final orders. She had seen Standish come forth with his little troop of horse, and thought how well both the men and their leaders looked. She beheld both parties pass through the gates, and for a moment lost sight of them, for they were hidden from view by the towers. Earnestly —most earnestly—did she pray for their success.

Gertrude looked on with equal interest, though feelings of a different kind agitated her breast, and her chief anxiety was for Standish. What would she have given to accompany him. Archdeacon Rutter regarded the sortie more calmly, but even he was deeply interested.

When next the watchers beheld the musketeers, they were marching swiftly, and in a compact body towards the trenches with Captain Chisenhale at their head, and Lieutenant Kay at the rear. Close behind rode Standish with his troop.

No sooner were they discovered by the sentinels, than the alarm was given, and several shots were fired against them.

But Chisenhale would not allow his men to return the fire. Hurrying forward as quickly as he could, he spread out his force, and quickly climbing the breastwork, poured a murderous fire into the trenches, killing a great number of the besiegers, and putting the rest to flight.

The fugitives, however, were intercepted by Standish, who had crossed with his men at a point not yet reached by the pioneers, and a sharp conflict ensued.

The Parliamentarians greatly outnumbered their assailants, and ought to have made a stand; but the furious onset of the Royalists proved irresistible.

With loud shouts of "For the king and the Earl of Derby!" they dashed among their opponents, hewing them down, or trampling them under foot.

Half a dozen prisoners were taken, and more than thrice that number of the rebels were killed—but not a single Royalist was wounded.

An hour had not elapsed since the sortie was made, and the victorious Royalists were returning to the castle with a great number of arms — swords, pistols, musquetoons, bandoleers, and match-tubes—a drum and a flag—together with the prisoners previously mentioned.

The triumphant issue of the conflict had

been witnessed with great exultation from the towers and ramparts of the mansion, and loud shouts hailed the victors on their return.

X.

OF THE IMPORTANT PRISONER BROUGHT IN BY STANDISH.

No one was more elated than the countess, though she veiled her satisfaction under a calm exterior.

Quitting the Eagle Tower, she repaired to the court-yard with her daughters and Gertrude, and arrived there just as Chisenhale and Standish entered the gate.

The services of Captain Ogle, who was waiting to cover their retreat, had not been required, but he was first to welcome them back.

By this time the court-yard was thronged. Major Farrington and all the officers not employed in the affair, had assembled to congratulate their friends on their success. The whole place resounded with shouts.

Standish and Chisenhale, with their two lieutenants, lost no time in presenting themselves to the countess, who was stationed near the entrance of the mansion, and received her congratulations and hearty thanks.

"You have indeed rendered me a most important service," she said; "and though I never doubted your courage and zeal, I scarcely thought it possible you could achieve so much."

"Our success is mainly owing to the bravery of our followers, who have displayed the greatest gallantry," said Captain Chisenhale. "They have given the rebels a lesson that will not easily be forgotten."

"I am proud of both officers and men —and with good reason," rejoined the countess. "As to you, Captain Standish, you have amply redeemed your promise, and have brought back both arms and prisoners."

"I have brought with me a far more important prisoner than I ever expected to capture," replied Standish.

"Indeed!" exclaimed the countess. "Where is he?"

"Yonder, with the others," replied Standish.

"They are all accoutred alike," said the countess. "I see no one who appears above the rank of a common soldier."

"Yet the ablest engineer in the service of the Parliament is amid the group," rejoined Standish.

"The ablest engineer!" exclaimed the countess in surprise. "That should be

Colonel Rosworm. You would not have me understand that he is a prisoner?"

Then calling to Gertrude, who was standing near, she said to her:

"Look at those men. Do you recognise any one of them?"

Gertrude remained silent.

"Is your father there?" pursued the countess. "Be not afraid to speak. No harm shall befall him."

"After that promise I will avow the truth," rejoined Gertrude. "He is there, madam."

"Bring Colonel Rosworm forward that I may question him," said the countess to Standish.

The injunction was obeyed, and in another moment the prisoner stood before her.

He maintained a very bold demeanour, and signed to his daughter, who would have rushed forward to him, to remain quiet.

"Do I behold Colonel Rosworm?" asked the countess. "If so, I may deem myself singularly fortunate."

"I am the person you suppose, madam," replied the prisoner. "I have no desire for concealment. I am certain I shall be honourably treated by your ladyship."

"You may rely on that, sir," she replied. "I bear you no personal enmity. Apart from your hostility to the king, I esteem your character, and I have the highest opinion of your skill as an engineer. But how is it that I see you in this disguise?"

"My buff coat is not intended as a disguise, madam," he replied. "I have doffed my cuirass and other accoutrements, in order that I might work more freely in the trenches. I did not expect to appear before your ladyship, or I would have come more suitably attired. But, in sooth, I had not time for any change of dress. When your musketeers climbed the breastwork, and fired into the trench, I cared not to tarry there, and had enough to do to save my life by flight. Having no arms to defend myself, I was subsequently taken prisoner by Captain Standish, but he did not demand my name."

"I knew you perfectly well, colonel, and deemed the inquiry unnecessary," remarked Standish. "But I had another reason for the course I pursued," he added, turning to the countess. "I wished to give your ladyship an agreeable surprise, and I think I have succeeded in my aim."

"You have," she observed, with a smile. "As to you, Colonel Rosworm, I am really glad to see you. You will be a prisoner on parole, and while you are detained here you shall not have to complain of harsh treatment. Till you are ransomed, or exchanged as a hostage of war, you shall have as much liberty as you can reasonably desire, and enjoy the society of your daughter."

"I thank your ladyship for your great consideration," replied Rosworm. "And I readily give you my word that I will not attempt to escape."

"Enough," said the countess. "Of necessity, you must submit to a certain restraint—but it shall not be much."

Any uneasiness that Gertrude might have felt was now completely dispelled. Coming forward she said to the countess:

"Am I at liberty to speak to my father, madam?"

"Assuredly," replied the countess. "It is my wish that you should be together as much as you please. Find a lodging for him forthwith. I commit him to your charge."

In another minute Gertrude and Rosworm had disappeared, but not till both had expressed their gratitude.

Most of those who witnessed this scene thought the countess showed far too much consideration to the German engineer; but Major Farrington, Archdeacon Rutter, and Standish regarded her conduct differently, and thought it exceedingly judicious.

The rest of the captives were not quite so fortunate. The countess did not deign to notice them. Taken to the gate-house, they were confined in the prison under the guard-room, there to remain till the chances of war might effect their liberation.

It will not be supposed that Lady Derby neglected to return thanks to Heaven for the success vouchsafed her. From the court-yard she proceeded to the chapel, whither all the officers and most of the men engaged in the sortie, followed her.

It was a service to be remembered, since there was one person present on the occasion, who could not have been looked for.

This was Rosworm. Probably Gertrude induced him to attend; but be that as it may, the countess was well pleased to behold him in the chapel.

XI.

HOW THE COUNTESS RECEIVED A VISIT FROM SEVERAL ROYALIST GENTLEMEN.

NEXT day, being Sunday, there was a suspension of hostilities, and no firing took place on either side.

It could not be discovered whether the enemy were at work in the trenches, but it seemed not, and it was certain the different parties of men collected near the tents were singing psalms, or listening to the lengthy discourses of their preachers, for their voices could be heard by the musketeers on the towers and gate-house, even at that distance.

If the besiegers were engaged in their devotions so were the besieged. Half the garrison attended divine service in the chapel at an early hour in the morning, and the remainder later on, when a thanksgiving sermon was preached by Archdeacon Rutter.

In the afternoon, an incident occurred for which the countess was quite unprepared.

She was in the great hall with her daughters and some other persons, when Major Farrington came to inform her that some half-dozen Royalist gentlemen, with whom she was well acquainted, had just arrived at the castle.

Scarcely able to credit the statement, she inquired who they were, and how it came to pass that they were permitted by the enemy to approach the gate.

"They have a safeguard from Sir Thomas Fairfax, who is desirous they should have an interview with your ladyship," replied Major Farrington; "as he hopes they may induce you to surrender the mansion."

"Methought you said they are Royalist gentlemen with whom I am well acquainted," remarked the countess. "They can know little of me, if they entertain any such notion. Who are they?"

"The principal person among them is Sir Thomas Prestwich," replied Major Farrington. "With him are Sir Edward Litten, Sir John Getherick, Mr. Gillibrand, Mr. Fleetwood, and Mr. Leigh—all adherents of the noble lord, your husband, and devoted to the royal cause."

"Bring them to me, I pray you," said

the countess. "I shall be glad to see them."

Shortly afterwards the gentlemen in question were ceremoniously ushered into the hall, and presented to her ladyship by Major Farrington, who received them very courteously.

"I am glad to see you, gentlemen," she said, "though I marvel you have been able to obtain admittance to me."

"We could not have done so, but for the consideration shown us by General Fairfax," replied Sir Thomas Prestwich. "We have a petition to your ladyship, signed by many friends and adherents of your noble husband, praying you to make terms with your enemies, who are disposed to treat you honourably and fairly, and not continue a useless resistance."

"I thank you, gentlemen, for the interest you take in me," she replied; "but you would have done better to petition those rebellious leaders who have plundered and spoiled the county to cease their wicked actions, rather than come to me, who seek to attack no one, but desire only to defend my children and my mansion during my lord's enforced absence. You profess yourselves loyal servants of the king, and I do not doubt your zeal, but see you not that you are taking part with his enemies in bringing this petition to me? It is the aim of Sir Thomas Fairfax and those with him to induce me to surrender. But they will fail. No representations, either of friend or foe, shall induce me to take such an unworthy course. I will make no terms with declared rebels and traitors, for those who are faithless to their sovereign are not likely to be true to me. You shall take no message back from me to Sir Thomas Fairfax, save one of defiance.

With Heaven's help I will hold my house against him and all my enemies, and he will never induce me to surrender, either by promises that I disbelieve, or threats that I despise. Take back this answer from me, I pray you, Sir Thomas, to General Fairfax, and say it is final. I will receive no more messages from him — nor would I have received this, had it not been brought by you."

"We applaud your resolution, madam," said Sir Thomas Prestwich. "You have entirely changed our sentiments. We were led to believe it would be impossible for you to hold out against the force brought against you, but we now think otherwise."

"Have you not heard of the success of our sortie yesterday, Sir Thomas?" asked Major Farrington. "We have made a most important prisoner. Colonel Rosworm is now in our hands."

"No mention was made to us of the circumstance," replied Prestwich. "The capture of Rosworm is indeed important."

"He is here," remarked Major Farrington. "Look towards the bottom of the hall, and you will behold him. You can now tell Sir Thomas Fairfax that you have seen him here."

"I shall not fail to do so," replied Prestwich. "We will now take our leave of your ladyship."

"Nay, you must not depart thus, gentlemen," she said. "Stay and dine with me, I pray you. You will then be able to tell Sir Thomas Fairfax that we do not lack provisions."

The party required little pressing, but willingly consented to stay.

Orders having been sent to the steward by Major Farrington, an abundant repast was speedily served, to which more than fifty persons, including the chaplains and officers, sat down.

Sir Thomas Prestwich and his companions were placed at the upper end of the table near the countess, and only separated from them by Doctor Brideoake was Colonel Rosworm.

In taking leave of her ladyship, her visitors bade her be of good cheer, and as they passed through the gate they called out "God bless the king and the Earl of Derby."

XII.

HOW ROSWORM WAS TAKEN BY STANDISH TO THE GUARD-ROOM IN THE GATE-HOUSE.

COLONEL ROSWORM seemed quite reconciled to his captivity. Indeed, there was nothing irksome about it, since he was treated rather as a guest than as a prisoner.

The countess directed Standish to show him every attention, and take him where he would, except upon the Eagle Tower and ramparts.

Rosworm had thus an opportunity of seeing the men, and was greatly struck by their appearance. Almost all of them were stalwart fellows with a very resolute expression of countenance, and though many of them were not equipped as soldiers, but looked like what they were—huntsmen, keepers, and fowlers—he could not doubt they were excellent marksmen, and admirably adapted for the service on which they were employed.

"Those men have been most judiciously chosen," he remarked to Standish; "and now I see them and their long fowling-pieces, I do not wonder that so many of our pioneers have been shot."

"I will show you some of our best marksmen," said Standish. "They have just finished their watch, and have gone into the guard-room. We shall find them there."

With this, he took Rosworm to the gate-house, near which half a dozen musketeers were posted, and entering a small door in one of the towers, mounted a short circular staircase that brought them to the guard-room.

A large square chamber, with strong stone walls, and a staircase on either side that afforded instant communication with the leads above on which two pieces of ordnance were placed.

Narrow loopholes commanded the drawbridge, and there was a mullioned window looking towards the outer court.

Within the chamber were machines for raising and lowering the two portcullises.

Seated on benches at a stout oak table, and making a hearty meal from a cold meat pasty were a dozen stalwart men. Occasionally they applied to a large jug of beer placed in the centre of the table, but these interruptions were not frequent.

All these individuals wore buff coats, and

belts from which hung powder-flasks and pouches containing bullets; while reared against the walls were long fowling-pieces and screwed guns evidently belonging to them.

So occupied were the hungry marksmen with their meal, that they did not notice the entrance of Standish and his companion; and besides, the intruders were partly hidden by the portcullis which had been raised.

"What hast thou done, Tom Thornhaugh?" asked a man whose back was towards them, of a brawny yeoman who sat opposite him. "I heard thee fire twice, and I suppose neither shot missed?"

"Thou art right, Dick Bold," replied Thornhaugh. "It grieves me to kill those poor country folk who are forced in the trenches—but I couldn't help it. I wish I could get a shot at some of their officers—

but they always contrive to keep out of reach."

"Not always," rejoined Dick Bold, with a laugh. "I should have lodged a bullet in Captain Bootle's brain this morning, had he not worn a combed head-piece."

"I have been on the look out for Colonel Rigby," remarked another, whose name appeared to be Launce Walker; "but he was too cautious to come near."

"Ay, marry, Rigby would have been a feather in thy cap, Launce," observed Dick Bold. "All the garrison would have rejoiced at his death, but thou say'st truly—he won't expose himself to danger."

"Nay, we ought to give the devil himself his due," observed another of the company. "Rigby doesn't want courage."

"He doesn't want cunning and malice," said Dick Bold. "I verily believe it is he who has caused this place to be besieged. He hates our good lord because he trailed his friend Captain Birch under a hay-cart at Manchester. That was a good jest."

"Ha! ha! ha!" laughed the whole company.

"I wish Captain Standish would make Rigby a prisoner in his next sally," remarked Thornhaugh.

"We have got a prisoner worth a dozen of Rigby," said Dick Bold.

"You mean Colonel Rosworm," remarked Launce Walker.

"Ay," rejoined Bold. "If he would only join us, we should have nothing to fear."

"We have nothing to fear as it is," said Launce. "But no doubt Rosworm could give us great help."

At this juncture the person referred to made a movement to depart.

"Let us go," he said. "I have played the listener too long."

But Standish detained him, and drew him forward.

As soon as the men became aware of Rosworm's presence they all arose.

"I have heard what you have just said," Rosworm remarked; "and I thank you for the good opinion you seem to entertain of me."

"Join us, colonel! join us!" they cried with one voice.

"No, I cannot do that," he replied. "But I will not fight against you if I can help it."

"You must not have the opportunity of doing so, colonel," said Standish. "Now you are here, we must keep you with us."

"Ay, that we must," cried the men.

"But the countess has promised to exchange me," rejoined Rosworm. "And you well know she will keep her word."

"Ay, if her ladyship has made you that promise no more need be said. But you may change your mind, colonel, and stay."

"I don't think that likely," he rejoined.

"Then we must try and prevent your departure," cried the men.

"I feel no apprehension on that score," laughed Rosworm, as he quitted the guard-room with Standish.

XIII.

IN WHAT MANNER A LETTER WAS SENT TO COLONEL ROSWORM.

As they returned through the court, they saw the countess and her daughters. She was attended by Major Farrington, Archdeacon Rutter, and one or two of the officers.

"I must now leave you," said Standish. "Her ladyship is about to ascend the Eagle Tower, and I must attend her."

"You should caution her not to expose herself too much," said Rosworm. "At present we have no cannon that can reach the summit of that tower—but some bombards and a culverin are expected."

"I will tell her what you say," rejoined Standish.

And he proceeded towards the entrance of the Eagle Tower.

Rosworm was still in the outer court, pacing to and fro, and thinking over what had just occurred, when a soldier halted beside him, and holding out his hand as he spoke, said, in a significant tone:

"I have just picked up this ball, colonel. Have you dropped it?"

Thus addressed, Rosworm looked at the man and saw that he held between his fingers and thumb, a wax ball about the size of a musket bullet.

"Give it me," he said, instantly comprehending what was meant.

The man complied, and without waiting to be thanked, marched on.

The incident did not occupy more than a minute, so that if noticed by the musketeers on the ramparts, it was not likely to excite suspicion.

Rosworm continued his promenade for a short time longer, and then repairing to his lodging, which was in an outbuilding attached to the mansion, he broke the ball, and found—as he expected—that it contained a letter, written on very thin paper.

He fancied the handwriting was that of Captain Bootle, but as the words were traced in pencil, he did not feel quite sure.

The message was very brief, and ran thus:

"Means will be found to effect your escape. Be prepared. You have a friend in the house."

"The offer is useless," mentally ejaculated Rosworm, after he had read the missive. "I have promised the countess not to attempt flight, and I cannot break my word."

While he was revolving the matter, a tap was heard at the door, and Gertrude entered the chamber.

"Do you find your captivity irksome, dear father?" she inquired. "You look melancholy."

"Were I not bound by my word, I need not remain here," he replied. "Means of escape have just been offered me. Read that letter:

After casting her eyes over it, Gertrude said:

"I will not ask how this letter was brought you, father," she said; "but I am sorry to find we have traitors in the castle."

"Those traitors are my friends," remarked Rosworm. "No word must be said of this matter to the countess."

"She ought to know it, father," rejoined Gertrude.

"She must not, child," said Rosworm, sternly, and authoritatively. "It is sufficient that I shall not avail myself of the offer made me."

"But by the same means which would be employed for your flight a secret communication may be kept up with the enemy."

"That cannot be helped," said her father.

"I do not feel that I shall be doing my duty to the countess by keeping silence, father."

"Your duty is to me, child. I lay my commands upon you. You will not dare to disobey them."

Well knowing that remonstrance would be useless, Gertrude did not attempt it, but she said:

"Would it were possible, father, that you could aid this noble lady to defend her mansion against the rebels!"

Rosworm shook his head, but his looks showed that her entreaties had produced some impression.

Seeing this, she flung herself on her knees before him, and exclaimed:

"I will not rise till you grant my prayer! Aid her, I implore you, dear father! aid her!"

"I cannot, daughter," replied Rosworm. "My sympathies are with her, but I must not—cannot aid her. Besides," he added, after a pause, "I do not think she needs assistance."

"You give me hopes," she cried, rising

to her feet. "You are of opinion that the countess will triumph?"

"From what I have seen since I came here I am convinced she can hold out till the Earl of Derby comes to her deliverance."

"May I tell her you have said so? It will give her hopes."

"As you please," he replied. "It is really my opinion."

Just then, the door was opened, and Standish entered the room.

"I bring you good news, Colonel Rosworm," he said. "You are no longer a prisoner."

"I will not suppose for a moment that you are jesting with me, Captain Standish," rejoined Rosworm. "But I am scarcely able to credit the intelligence."

"What has happened?" asked Gertrude, equally astonished.

"Your father has been ransomed," replied Standish. "A letter has just been brought from Sir Thomas Fairfax, offering a large sum as a ransom for Colonel Rosworm, and the countess has accepted the offer. You are therefore free, and can return with the messenger. Her ladyship has sent me to convey the intelligence to you, well knowing the errand would be agreeable to me."

"I thank you heartily, Captain Standish," rejoined Rosworm. "The intelligence is wholly unexpected on my part, for I need scarcely say I have had no communication with Sir Thomas Fairfax, and I did not think he valued my services so highly as to offer a ransom for my liberation."

"Then you will depart at once, father," cried Gertrude, "and again join the ranks of the enemy."

"I shall not depart without taking leave of the countess," rejoined Rosworm, "and thanking her for the generous treatment I have experienced."

"Her ladyship has descended from the Eagle Tower, and is now on the parade," said Standish. "I will conduct you to her."

Having no preparations to make for his departure, Rosworm at once accompanied Standish to the outer court, where they found the countess and her usual attendants.

At some little distance stood the Parliamentary officer who had brought the message from Sir Thomas Fairfax.

"Colonel Rosworm is come to take leave of your ladyship," said Standish, leading the somewhile prisoner forward.

Rosworm bowed deeply, and in accents that bespoke his sincerity, thanked the countess for the great kindness she had shown him.

"Rarely has a prisoner of war been treated as I have been," he said; "and I shall ever entertain a grateful sense of your ladyship's kindness. But I fear I shall never be able to requite it. May I ask if you have made any stipulations in regard to my release?"

"None whatever," she replied. "You are free to act as you think proper. Had I made any bargain I would have consulted you."

"Such noble conduct is worthy of you, madam," said Rosworm. "You set an example to your enemies which they will do well to follow."

With another profound salutation, he turned to depart.

After bidding adieu to his daughter, he joined the officer, who was waiting for him, and they were conducted by Standish and a guard to the gate.

On the way hither, they encountered Captain Chisenhale and Captain Ogle. Both of them bowed to him and the former remarked:

"We shall be glad to see you here again, colonel, in the same character."

In another minute Rosworm had passed through the wicket at the side of the gate, crossed the drawbridge, and was riding with the messenger and a sergeant who had accompanied him on his errand towards the camp.

On the way thither, he looked back once or twice at the beleaguered mansion, but made no remark, nor did he answer any questions put to him by his companion.

XIV.

A TRAITOR PUNISHED.

A MIST rendered it very dark that night, and one of the sentinels stationed on the ramparts at the back of the castle, fancying he heard some one swimming across the moat, fired in the direction of the sound, but missed his aim owing to the obscurity.

It was subsequently discovered that one of the soldiers—the same who had delivered the secret letter to Rosworm—had got out at the postern gate, and favoured by the darkness had effected his escape in the manner described.

This circumstance being mentioned to Standish, caused him some uneasiness, for though he could not account for the man's flight at that juncture, he felt certain he was a traitor.

After some discussion with Captain Chisenhale and Lieutenant Bretergh, these two officers resolved to anticipate any attack that might be made by the enemy, and give them another alarm in the trenches.

Accordingly, about an hour later, accompanied by thirty musketeers, they proceeded to the postern tower, part of which stood on the further side of the moat, and beyond the palisades, and issuing forth from a small door strongly cased with iron, marched swiftly and silently towards the trenches.

But they were not so successful as on the previous occasion. The enemy were more on the alert, and had placed sentinels on the breastwork.

Though these men could not distinguish the sallying party, they were warned of their approach by the lighted matches carried by the musketeers, and gave the alarm; whereupon their comrades instantly quitted the trenches, and speeded towards an adjoining wood; whither they were chased by Chisenhale and his company.

Sheltered by the trees, the fugitives sustained little loss, and only three or four were killed.

One prisoner was likewise made, and this proved to be Ralph Thorold, the man who had just escaped from the garrison.

When brought back to the mansion, and interrogated by Major Farrington, Thorold confessed that he had been in communication with Captain Bootle, but refused to declare how the letters had been brought to him.

Adjudged to die the death of a traitor, he was hanged at an early hour next morning from the battlements of the postern tower in full view of the trenches.

XV.

HOW A LETTER SENT BY THE EARL OF DERBY TO FAIRFAX WAS BROUGHT BY CAPTAIN ASHHURST TO THE COUNTESS.

NEXT morning, Captain Ashhurst rode with a flag of truce to the gates of the castle, and sought an interview of the countess; stating that he had an important message to deliver to her from Sir Thomas Fairfax.

Though wearied out with propositions ending in nothing, her ladyship consented to receive him, and the messenger was conducted by Standish to the presence-chamber, where he found her with Major Farrington and Archdeacon Rutter.

Captain Ashhurst's manner was extremely respectful, and offered a marked contrast to the insolent deportment that generally characterised a Parliamentary officer.

Bowing to the countess, he informed her that Sir Thomas Fairfax had just received a despatch from the Earl of Derby, and had sent it for her perusal."

"It is here, madam," he continued, handing it to her, "and it is the general's opinion that this letter will have more weight with you than any message he could send."

"Let me see it," said the countess. "Ay, truly, it is from my lord, and sent from Castle Rushen."

And she could not help pressing her lips to the signature.

Seeing her so much moved, Captain Ashhurst augured well for the success of his mission.

But as she read the letter, her aspect entirely changed, and she looked stern and resolved.

After showing the letter to her advisers, who returned it without a word, she said:

"His lordship writes in error. Unaware of the propositions already made by Sir Thomas Fairfax, and of my rejection of them, he desires an honourable and free passage for myself and my children, being unwilling to expose us to the danger and suffering of a lengthened siege."

"Exactly so, madam," replied Captain Ashhurst; "and I am instructed by Sir Thomas Fairfax to say that if your ladyship wills it, he will readily grant his lordship's request."

"Tell Sir Thomas Fairfax I am much

beholden to him for his consideration in referring the matter to me," she rejoined. "But I must beg that he will henceforth treat with my lord. When I receive my husband's express commands I will obey them, be they what they may. But till I am assured that his lordship desires me to yield up this castle, I will neither quit it, nor make any terms for its surrender."

Both Major Farrington and Doctor Rutter looked at her approvingly, but neither spoke.

"Pardon me, madam," said Captain Ashhurst, "if I venture to observe that the Earl of Derby's wishes are plainly conveyed in this letter. Had not his lordship felt that you ought to surrender, he would not have written in these terms to the general. For that reason Sir Thomas has sent you the letter."

"And I thank him again for his courtesy,

and for choosing you as his messenger," replied the countess. "Take back the letter to your general, and tell him that till I learn my lord's pleasure I shall abide where I am, and wait the event in full confidence of Heaven's support."

Seeing that the audience was at an end, Ashhurst retired, and was conducted to the gate by Standish.

"Yours is a noble lady," he said; "and it is impossible not to sympathise with her. For her own sake I wish she would surrender."

"She has nothing to fear," rejoined Standish.

XVI.

HOW TWO PIECES OF ORDNANCE WERE SEIZED BY STANDISH.

On that night, despite a constant fire from the postern tower, the besiegers contrived to bring up a demi-cannon and a culverin, and placed them on the summit of the rising ground beyond the moat.

Next morning the cannoniers on the opposite towers tried ineffectually to dislodge these pieces of ordnance. Several shots were fired from the newly-erected battery against the walls of the mansion, but without doing any material damage.

Afterwards a higher range was taken. Two or three battlements were broken, and a musketeer who imprudently showed himself on the ramparts was killed.

This was regarded as a great achievement by the enemy, who raised a loud shout; but their exultation was soon over, for within a quarter of an hour two of the cannoniers were killed.

Another sortie was made that night by Standish and Chisenhale, accompanied by fifty musketeers—their object being to dismount the two pieces of cannon that had given the garrison so much trouble throughout the day. After a sharp conflict with the guard, during which Captain Chisenhale was slightly wounded, they succeeded in accomplishing their design.

Their triumph would have been complete, if they could have brought the two guns away with them, but this was impracticable.

The besiegers now began to show more activity and determination than they had hitherto displayed.

Provoked at the destruction of their little battery, they brought up a basilisk and a saker, two pieces of ordnance of smaller calibre than a culverin, and planted them against the gate-towers.

A misdirected shot from the basilisk entered the wicket, and killed one of the guard, but did not find its way to the court.

Immediately afterwards the gate was thrown open, and the drawbridge lowered, and a party of horsemen headed by Standish dashed out provided with ropes.

Seizing the two pieces of ordnance, they dragged them into the court, their own retreat being covered by the guns in the gate-towers.

Not a single man was lost on the occasion.

Hitherto, the Royalists had been uniformly successful, and had baffled all the attempts of the enemy, generally inflicting severe loss upon them.

But it was felt that these constant defeats would only make the besiegers more determined, and that their efforts to take the mansion would be redoubled.

The besieged had no fear of such a result, but to prevent it the utmost vigilance and activity were required.

XVII.

OF THE PREPARATIONS MADE FOR A GRAND SORTIE.

By this time the works of the besiegers had made great progress. Bulwarks had been cast up, but as yet all the batteries had not been mounted with cannon.

It was also certain that a mine had been commenced, which it was intended should pass under the moat, either for the purpose of blowing up some of the towers, or cutting off the water.

As the deep well from which the garrison was abundantly supplied was situated in the very centre of the castle, it would necessarily take the miners some time to reach it, and it was resolved to sink a countermine to meet them as soon as their course could be discovered.

Engineers were, therefore, posted in various places to listen for any sounds that might guide them in their task.

Notwithstanding all these disquieting circumstances the courage of the countess remained unshaken, and, indeed, rose higher than ever. Nor was uneasiness manifested by any one in the mansion. Even those not engaged in its defence were full of ardour.

But the person most interested in the siege was Gertrude. As we have shown, she took an active part in the defence of the house —carried messages and orders—mounted ramparts and towers—and watched the cannonier when he pointed his gun, and would have done more if she had been permitted. Her great desire was to attend a sortie, and she would have accompanied the first expedition habited in male attire, if the countess would have allowed her.

With this recklessness, she now passed hours in the postern-tower, accounted the most dangerous part of the castle, being most exposed to a sudden assault of the enemy. Here she could watch the progress of their fortifications, and could count the sakers, the periers, the minions, and falconets on their batteries.

One morning while engaged in her survey she perceived that the besiegers had begun a new fort on which they were most diligently employed.

Fixed on the summit of a rising ground at a short distance on the south-west, it commanded the whole of the mansion ; but the position being too high for cannon, it was evident the battery was intended for a mortar, or a bombard. The sconce was circular, and surrounded by a rampart, which, as yet, was unfinished.

On making this discovery, Gertrude hastened to the countess, but her ladyship had already been informed of the new fort by Major Farrington and Standish, and had given orders that it should be destroyed, if possible.

Accordingly the cannoniers had just opened fire, and having killed two of the men, and driven away the rest, were knocking down the ramparts.

"We may check the work for a time," said Standish. "But it is certain it will be resumed on the first opportunity."

"No doubt the sconce is designed for the

large mortar, with which we have been threatened," observed Major Farrington.

"The monster shall be silenced as soon as he begins to roar," said Standish. "Meantime, we must make another sortie, and destroy the works. The enemy have been too long unmolested, and have grown insolent."

"I approve of your design," said the countess. "But this time, you must take a large party with you, and do the work effectually. How say you, sir?" she added, to Major Farrington. "I think half the garrison should go forth on this occasion."

"I am quite of your ladyship's opinion," replied Farrington. "We must inflict a blow upon them, calculated to shake their overweening confidence."

"True," rejoined the countess. "The near approach of those forts and batteries is unpleasant to me. You must give Captain Standish the command of this expedition."

"In an affair of this kind, wherein so large a number of men will be concerned, more than one leader will be required," said Major Farrington. "I therefore propose—with your ladyship's approval—to divide the party into three squadrons—one squadron to be commanded by Captain Standish, another by Captain Farmer, and the third by Captain Molineux Radcliffe. This will prevent any jealousy."

"You are right," said the countess. "And I trust Captain Standish is satisfied with the arrangement."

"Perfectly," he replied. "I could desire no better."

"Each officer can take his own lieutenant," pursued Major Farrington.

"Mine shall be Bretergh," cried Standish

"I propose to make several other arrangements within the mansion," said Major Farrington. "But before doing so, I desire to consult your ladyship."

"Let me hear them," she rejoined.

"First then, at the gates, which must be kept open, and the drawbridge down, I shall station Captain Ogle and a party of musketeers to defend the entrance. Should the enemy approach—though I do not deem it likely—the cannoniers will fire upon them from the towers and gate-house. The sally-port in the postern-tower shall be guarded by Captain Chisenhale with a party of men ready to succour our friends should they need aid. Captain Rawsthorne shall have charge of the musketeers upon the walls, while Captain Foxe shall be posted on the summit of the Eagle Tower, and with a pair of flags signal the movements of the enemy—so that our friends may know when to advance or retire."

"Your plan seems well considered," remarked the countess; "and if fully carried out, as I doubt not it will be, cannot fail to be successful. I have always thought that signals might be given from the Eagle Tower. I will be there myself. And you shall attend me, if you will, damsel," she added to Gertrude.

"Your ladyship could not confer a greater favour upon me," was the reply.

Soon afterwards, Major Farrington and Standish quitted the countess to make preparations for the proposed sortie.

Though the utmost activity prevailed within the garrison, no sign of it was manifest to the enemy, who began to think the besieged had taken alarm and were meditating a surrender. The besiegers therefore resumed the work they had suspended, and repaired the damage done to the sconce, intending to play the mortar with stones of eighty pounds weight on the following day.

END OF VOL. II.

LONDON:
PRINTED BY C. WHITING, BEAUFORT HOUSE, DUKE STREET,
LINCOLN'S-INN-FIELDS.

www.ingramcontent.com/pod-product-compliance
Lightning Source LLC
Chambersburg PA
CBHW032056220426
43664CB00008B/1023